GOING GRAY

GOING GRAY

What I Learned about Beauty, Sex, Work,
Motherhood, Authenticity, and Everything
Else That Really Matters

Anne Kreamer

LITTLE, BROWN AND COMPANY

New York | Boston | London

Little, Brown and Company
Hachette Book Group USA
237 Park Avenue, New York, NY 10017
Visit our Web site at www.HachetteBookGroupUSA.com

First Edition: September 2007

The excerpt from the editor's letter by Peggy Northrop on page 133 is from the June 2006 issue of *More*. Reprinted with permission. The excerpt from Anderson Cooper on pages 168–169 is from the August 2003 issue of *Details*. Reprinted with permission.

Library of Congress Cataloging-in-Publication Data
Kreamer, Anne.
  Going gray : what I learned about beauty, sex, work, motherhood, authenticity, and everything else that really matters / Anne Kreamer.—1st ed.
    p. cm.
    ISBN 0-316-16661-8 / 978-0-316-16661-4
1. Middle-aged women—Biography. 2. Aging—Social aspects. 3. Gray hair. I. Title.
  HQ1059.4.K74 2007
  306.4'613—dc22   2007016435

10 9 8 7 6 5 4 3 2 1

Q-MART

Printed in the United States of America

For Kurt

Contents

How One Hair-Color Fiend Decides to Get Real   3

Only Her Hairdresser Knows for Sure   31

Hello? Your Roots Are *Really* Showing—
My Bad Hair Year   47

My Mother, Myself, My Daughters—
How We Decide How We Want to Look   68

Can Gray Be Sexy?   73

"Dating"—My Three-City Match.com Road Test   85

A Night on the Town   97

Is Gray Hair Illegal in Hollywood?   107

Red, White, and Blue, but Seldom Gray   119

Nine to Five   126

It's Not the Gray, It's the Clothes   139

The Slippery Slope   156

Contents

It's a Guy Thing, Too   168

Figuring Out Where You Stand —
The Fountain of Youth Index   175

French Women Do Go Gray   182

Is Gray the New Black?   191

Really Letting Go   196

Acknowledgments   205

People in this country are starved for the truth.

—Harry G. Frankfurt,
author of *On Bullshit* and *On Truth*

GOING GRAY

How One Hair-Color Fiend
Decides to Get Real

IN OCTOBER 2004, my friend, the artist Maira Kalman, sent me the photographs from a larkish summer driving trip that she, another friend, the writer Akiko Busch, my daughter Kate*, and I had taken to Lily Dale, New York, the oldest spiritualist community in America. Lily Dale was founded in 1879, and each summer the hundreds of resident psychics and mediums open their candy-colored, slightly down-on-its-heels Victorian town in western New York to the public. The Lily Dale Assembly Web site defines a spiritualist as "one who believes, as the basis of his or her religion, in the continuity of life and in individual responsibility. Some, but not all, Spiritualists are Mediums and/or Healers. Spiritualists endeavor to find the truth in all things and to live their lives in accordance therewith."

*With the exception of members of my family, people mentioned in the book without surnames are pseudonymous.

3

Certainly none of our summer group would have listed ourselves as "spiritualists" on an official form. We're really not, in a word, kooks. But we do like to think of ourselves as people groping toward the useful truths, and the chance to spend a long weekend together in rural New York, having our fortunes told, felt like the kind of trip that would be tremendous fun. And boy, were we right. We tried everything available to us in Lily Dale: communed with our fellow travelers in the mornings at the "Stump," a group session deep in the woods; had several individual sessions in psychics' homes; and participated in "healing ceremonies" in "temples."

We even got to mingle with a group of sixteen visiting Tibetan monks who were stopping in Lily Dale as part of a tour sponsored by Richard Gere, but regrettably none of the four of us experienced anything approximating a "visitation," nor were we blown away by any blinding moments of insight from a psychic.

But months later, as I looked through Maira's photographs, one in particular—of my sixteen-year-old daughter; Aki; and me—*actually changed my life.* In that instant, sandwiched between my blond daughter and gray-haired Aki, I saw myself for what I truly was: a forty-nine-year-old mother with a much too darkly shellacked helmet of hair. I clearly was not some faintly with-it older pal of my daughter's, but neither did my hair make me look like a contemporary of Aki's. It was like I was some spectral person floating in a no-man's-land, neither young nor old. I felt as if I didn't know who I really was.

In fact, as I studied the photo, I felt like I was a black hole between gaily dressed Kate and about-to-burst-into-laughter Aki. My uniform of deep, dark mahogany hair and dark clothing sucked all light out of my presence. Seeing that person—that version of myself—was like a kick to my solar plexus. In one second, all my years of careful artifice, attempting to preserve what I thought of as a youthful look, were ripped away. All I saw was a kind of confused, schlubby middle-aged woman with hair dyed much too harshly.*

BUT WHY THIS SUDDEN self-critical revelation? In the past, when I'd looked at photographs of myself, I'd always thought I'd looked pretty good. Maybe the portals to greater awareness had been subtly awakened at Lily Dale...? *Ummm, no.* I think I was just lucky that Maira's photo allowed me the momentary objectivity to see that the dyed-hair forty-nine-year-old wasn't the *real* me. Kate looked real. Aki looked real. To me, I looked like I was pretending to be someone I wasn't. Someone still young.

I had never before closely considered what the color of my hair communicated to the world. Artificial color was simply what I had always done, what almost everyone my age did, and what I unthinkingly assumed looked good.

But examining that snapshot made me start to think hard about who I was, and who I wanted to be. Would I continue holding on to some dream of youthfulness or could I end the game of denial and move more honestly into middle age?

*If you'd like to see this photo, go to www.AnneKreamer.com/book.html.

So maybe the trip to Lily Dale really had, after all, led me to try and "live my life in more accordance with the truth." I had gone on the trip for fun, as an exercise in anthropological tourism, wondering if I might, and rather credulously hoping to, for instance, receive a "message" from my dead parents. Instead of taking a mystical or metaphysical leap into a spiritual unknown, I found that looking at Maira's photograph led me to do something extremely concrete and practical. I came away from that trip with a decision to try to embrace more authenticity and, as a first step along that path, to do something as banal as to quit coloring my hair. To let it be whatever color it was — nickel? steel? charcoal? platinum? white? who knew? — beneath the dye. Beyond the inspired lunge toward more everyday personal candor, I was also simply curious about what I actually looked like.

For years, people had commented generously that my relatively unlined skin made me look young. I'm not fat. I don't often wear matronly clothes. *You don't look your age,* people told me. Naturally, I chose to believe them. And to tell the honest truth, in the self-image I cooked up in my brain, I even one-upped them: in my mind's eye, I imagined I looked thirty-five, not forty-nine. Wrong. I mean, *really wrong,* but there you are.

I grew up in white, upper-middle-class, suburban Kansas City, Missouri, during the '60s. In 1964 my parents took the family to the world's fair in New York City, where I experienced for the first time the dense electricity of real urbanity. I loved everything about New York: the crowds on the streets, the multiplicity of signs and architecture and styles of dress, the acrid and fishy smell of Chinatown, the *Jetsons*-like General Motors "Futurama" exhibit at the fair, even the spicy food (garlic!).

When the *Mod Squad* television series premiered in 1968, it represented that same quintessential urban coolness to me. It felt like my personal window into an adult world, where people of different classes and races worked together, and even though, as cops, the characters were "the man," they were also anti–everything establishment. Peggy Lipton, the lead actress, wore great clothes and had straight, long blond hair. And she got to hang out on camera with sexy Michael Cole and the grooviest of all, Clarence Williams III. I wanted to be Peggy Lipton much more than the other fantasy TV version of "me," Marcia Brady from *The Brady Bunch.*

In reality, I was a nerd (the girls in high school nicknamed me "Miss Organization," and I don't think they were envious), so having hair that made me seem like the kind of girl one saw on television was very important to me. I discovered that my hair was the one thing that I could manipulate to make me seem at least superficially like someone I wasn't.

So in high school, to try to be "cool" — that is, to look a little bit older, a little bit more sophisticated — I grew my hair long and styled it just like Peggy Lipton's. I also tried somewhat successfully to make my tawny hair even blonder by spritzing it with Sun In and lemon juice as I toasted during the hot Midwestern summers. Lightening the color was my second step in changing my hair to create a new, improved version of myself to project to the world.

As a teenager my salient physical attributes were my hair and my—"no, really, I'm *not* a nerd" additional bit of '70s pre-Goth rebellion—black nails. And although mercifully I jettisoned the black nail polish in college, as an adult the long, straight hairstyle I'd so carefully adopted in high school remained a defining piece of my look, inextricably linked with my identity—as, I think, our particular style does for nearly all of us. Subconsciously, I believe, I thought my hair possessed almost talismanic protective properties.

But even as I maintained the uniform length of my hair, I began further experimentation with its color as a tool to assert my individuality and uniqueness. And over the years, my hair has gone through many, many different hues, from what I thought of as aubergine—but which a male lawyer friend once horrifyingly described as "deep purple"—to various roan and chestnut shades.

My first job right out of college was as an administrative assistant at the now defunct Manufacturer's Hanover Bank, assigned to move money among the bank's clients in the Great Lakes District. Yes, it was in midtown Manhattan, but could there have been a more boring job in the world? I sat at a desk opposite the men's room in the front row of a vast airplane hangar–like open office space. (Trust me: there was nothing more mortifying for the twenty-one-year-old me than to have men by the dozen smile directly at me as they zipped their pants on leaving the bathroom.) My work consisted in its entirety of writing out paper-money wire-transfer requests for companies in Illinois and Indiana; robots could have handled the job. Row upon row of hushed, uptight people cascaded behind me in desk after desk, each row representing a notch up the hierarchy toward the glassed-in aquarium-like offices of the vice presidents. The few women who worked there in 1977 were blond and wore conservative suits and pumps. Wearing any style outside of the dull Brooks Brothers dress code was practically a fireable offense, so I dyed my hair a rich bittersweet color as a way to demonstrate to myself and to the outside world that I did not really belong in this death-before-my-time job. I thought the artificial color communicated that I was, like, you know, some kind of an *artist* who was working this job just to pay the rent. Which was true, minus the artist part.

I didn't stop using my hair color as a tool to differentiate myself after I quit the bank. My next job was as a secretary in the international division of Children's Television Workshop. And even though I wasn't doing anything other than taking dictation from an amped-up, full-of-himself, would-be-James-Bond British salesman, I wanted to try on a more sophisticated persona than my kind of down-market-bank-clerk reddish hue, so I colored my hair a rich walnut shade. And I actually felt different. More sophisticated. By the time I started traveling for the job, selling *Sesame Street* in Haiti and Brunei and Malaysia, I already felt a bit like Mata Hari (and you know what the anagram of her surname is, don't you?).

I discovered that the personality-enhancing aspect of my hair extended well beyond a sense of theatrical role-playing. I found that if I felt depressed, I could go and brighten up the hue and actually make myself feel brighter. When I felt like I wasn't getting enough attention from my boyfriend (and future husband), I could shift my color and, in my mind's eye, become instantly more alluring. I'm not so sure that this strategy actually worked, but it always made me feel as if I were taking control. There was nothing like transforming myself overnight from redhead to brunette or back again to make me feel like a new person. It was a regular cosmetic rebooting.

Hair color was something I could control easily, definitively—managing the color of my hair was my equivalent to taking Paxil. I discovered that when I changed my hair color, *voilà,* I'd move on—imagining, *hoping,* that by modifying the way I presented myself to the world, I was somehow actually *dealing* with whatever issues or uncertainties were confronting me at the moment.

On my fortieth birthday, in some I-want-to-be-a-rock-star-and-I'm-not-getting-older moment of fantastic denial, I indulged in my most dramatic and least successful coloring episode. I dyed my hair jet-black. Other than a few dutiful years of piano lessons, I'd never been musical—never played an instrument or sung in any kind of group. But at forty I chose to become thoroughly depressed over the fact that *now* I knew I would never become a Beatle. Yes, a Beatle. Insane in several respects? Yes! But at age nine in 1965, I'd seen them play live in my hometown, Kansas

City. That scene—teenagers gone wild, and sexy, sophisticated, *foreign* boys (with cool, long dark hair) being adored—became my benchmark (other than *The Mod Squad*) for a certain kind of glam living, one that would lead me out of my suburban Midwestern tapioca life.

But my 1995 fake-rocker black hair didn't, of course, magically deliver me a recording contract or global adoration. Rather, it served to underscore my true age in unattractive ways—the black washed me out and added gray shadows to my face. My friend Larry Doyle, who's a comedy writer, announced in his deadpan fashion the moment he saw me, "You look like your evil twin." And both of my children, then five and seven, actually cried the evening I came home with the new color. Not precisely my goal.

I lived with that mistake for a long time because you cannot simply wash ebony color out of your hair. As an emergency remedial adaptation, I went back and had my colorist layer mahogany dye into the black and then, chastened by the entire experiment, settled into a conservative, acceptable, middle-aged brownish.

And from then on I went on absolute hair-color autopilot, the opposite of my previous decade or so of flagrant dabbling. My forties' hair strategy became all about maintaining the status quo—consistent hair color meant nothing in my life was really changing. No aging, no anxiety I couldn't deal with, no friends divorcing or family members and friends dying... *everything was just fine.*

Until I looked hard at that photograph three years ago and everything wasn't fine, at least not as far as the way I looked was concerned.

Even though I've never once fudged my age, I simply wasn't prepared to *look* my age. And I thought that if I had my natural hair color, whatever it might be, I'd instantly look older. What was the big deal about looking my age? This was the real crux of my dilemma in wanting to present a more authentic version of myself to the world. At least since the flappers of the 1920s, we've valued extravagant youthfulness as the embodiment of all that is American—new nation, new ideals, youthful optimism and can-do-ism, Lindy Hopping and Boogalooing and Frugging our way through life to keep refreshing the sense that we are always creating ourselves anew. Even if we aren't. By keeping my gray "secret," not allowing my hair to visibly age, I was able to feel permanently thirty-four.

It never occurred to me that my light-sucking fake dark-brown hair might have had a subtle but even more profound aging effect. I chose not to register the fact that hair dye, inevitably, faintly stains the skin around the hairline, tipping off anyone who looks closely that what you are presenting is a simulation of youth.

As I approached fifty, I realized I was exhausted by the tyrannical upkeep, the enormous investment of time and money, just to seem younger—or at least not older. I was married, I was self-employed, my kids were almost adults. That equation no longer computed.

So how hideous could my natural color be—*whatever* it was—compared to liberation?

WHEN I HAD FIRST NOTICED gray hairs in my late twenties, I didn't give a second thought to covering them up. After all, I was already manipulating my color for professional/fantasy reasons, and frankly I thought twenty-seven was way too young to have gray hair. (From trying to look older in high school to trying to look younger at work just a decade later—such are the vicissitudes of a woman's life.) But at twenty-seven, in 1983, I didn't have much money, so I went with what I thought was the easy route to covering my gray—single-process coloring.

"Single process" is the technique whereby a coloring paste is applied to the scalp and roots with something like a pastry brush, forming a gooey helmet. (Ironic, isn't it, that this means of sexiness enhancement is so thoroughly unsexy: you never want any man who isn't a hair-care professional to see you looking like you've just climbed out of the La Brea tar pits.) It takes about forty minutes for the color to "set" from start to finish and, with shampoo and tips, costs about $125 at a midrange New York hair salon. (For those who do single process out of a box at home, the expense is a fraction of that, of course.) For highlighting, one's roots are treated with the single-process method, and then individual strands of hair are painted with a different bleaching chemical and folded into squares of foil. It's much more time-consuming—up to three hours—and, since it is virtually impossible to do at home, requires expensive ($200 and up) salon visits.

Either way, once you start coloring at thirty or thirty-five or forty—the insidious creep of roots perpetually growing out, lighter or darker, always threatening to show themselves and expose the ruse—you are trapped on a treadmill.

And the treadmill accelerates as you age. Particularly during the last ten years, as my roots became grayer and my artificial hair color ever darker, I found I needed to return to my colorist every two and a half weeks to keep my brown hair looking as spiffy as I'd come to demand—I didn't trust the at-home root-touch-up kits to look "natural." I couldn't bear even the teensiest millimeter of ratty gray roots showing, not just because I cared that people would consciously notice that I dyed my hair—over the years some of the colors I'd chosen had been obviously fake—but because the hard line between the visible gray roots and dyed dark parts looked ugly and losery to me.

I was more than a little nervous to share my decision to quit dyeing my hair with Joseph Artale, the owner of Arte, the low-key boutique salon in Manhattan's NoHo where my whole family has had their hair done for years. I wasn't afraid Joe would have a reality-TV kind of hissy fit over the notion. He's a sensible, well-adjusted, handsome father of three, and the whole vibe of his salon is chic but down-to-earth, intimate, familylike. But he was, after all, the professional, and I was worried that I might be making a mistake.

Joe only half-jokingly remarked, "Oh, God, I hope you don't start some kind of *trend* here." And then, in a more earnest and even slightly panicky way, he added, "Warning—this path not recommended for everyone." The salon business, of course, would be decimated if significant numbers of women stopped coloring their hair. But he was game.

I HAD NO REAL IDEA what I was getting into. I am an impulsive, ready-fire-aim person, and over the years I've come to realize that the best way for me to succeed at difficult tasks I've set for myself—quitting cigarettes, changing careers from magazine executive to TV producer to magazine writer and author, helping to start new businesses (*Spy* magazine in the 1980s, *Nickelodeon* magazine in the early '90s, a production company in the late '90s), selling a beloved farm in upstate New York—is to tell as many people as possible as quickly as I can about my plans. The public knowledge becomes a goad to keep me on track.

Even before telling my family that I'd decided to let my hair return to its natural color, I sought what I assumed would be positive reinforcement of my decision from a few friends my age. The results were mixed.

One of the first people I called to discuss my decision to allow my natural color to grow in was a childhood friend living in Lawrence, Kansas. Jane was on the same page. She told me that she'd recently had her hair guy begin to transition her blond highlights to white ones. She made me laugh aloud when she said, "I'm hoping it grows out that beautiful snow color, but I fear it'll be more like old-lady pubes. But hey, Emmylou rocks! My husband is totally hot for her." And like all good friends, she encouraged me. "You're going to be one of those fabulous-looking white-haired women in great scarves and sweaters over cigarette-leg pants." Her instant feedback was inspiring. I thought, *Yes, exactly, sophisticated and cool* and *part of a movement.*

My gray-haired friends—a tiny minority of women I know, maybe 5 percent—were, like members of all "clubs" who want new converts, extremely enthusiastic. Aki, one of my Lily Dale traveling companions who swims seriously and doesn't color partly because her hair would turn a martian chartreuse in the chlorine, promised that it would feel liberating, a release from a minor but real tyranny. Two women in my book club, both in their midsixties with fabulous white hair, said they'd seldom been happier than in the days after they decided to quit coloring. *Okay,* I thought, *I can do this.* I had positive role models whom I respected and thought were sexy and reasonably content.

A friend in her early fifties who's recovering from cancer had an even more important take for me. "My hair has grown in postchemo very gray," she said, "and I'm thinking of keeping it that way. It's for a sort of show-offy reason. I like telling people that, because of this cancer, I've seen my own ghost. Even though I wish I could say I turned gray overnight, my hair didn't actually turn white from fear"—for years she had dyed it brown—"but its whiteness symbolizes having been terrified. On a simpler level, I like the before-and-after quality of it. I'm not the same person

I was before I got sick. I've been through some sort of crucible. It's a kind of badge of…well, not of courage but of having been changed, like being a veteran of a war." I realized after talking with her that I'd rather be allied with a woman like that—someone who had faced the ultimate challenge and come out stronger on the other side—than pretend as if everything were coming up roses all the time.

On the other hand, I was given pause when I read that the musician Melissa Etheridge, after finishing her cancer treatment and making her brave and bald Grammy appearance, said, "I have a beautiful head of hair…I do dye it blond, though. I can be bald in front of the world, but I can't be gray." If a strong, outspoken feminist was scared to stop coloring, what was I letting myself in for?

When I started sharing the plan with friends who colored their hair, the feedback I got was more varied, in many ways interesting but not exactly encouraging.

Some went into great detail about their own private daydreams of giving up hair color. One friend, who had dabbled extensively in cosmetic procedures—liposuction, Botox, fillers, a nose job—told me that she wanted to be able to stop worrying about *all of it.* But she said she lacked the courage to try.

Other women were simply astonished and appalled. *"What?"* my sexy, fiftysomething, "blond" Italian American housewife neighbor shouted when I mentioned my decision. "Why *on earth* would you want to make yourself look *older?"* And rather shockingly to me, a very good friend—proud old-school feminist and

liberal, successful media executive—echoed that same sentiment. "I just can't imagine what would motivate you to do this.
I intend to keep coloring my hair until I drop."

When I shared my decision to go gray with my friend Nora
Ephron, unaware that she was in the middle of writing her de-
lightful, smart *I Feel Bad About My Neck: And Other Thoughts on
Being a Woman,* she had a ready reply, cool and sharp. She'd
clearly thought a lot about this. "Having gray hair is a political
act for some people. They lend a lot of priority to the *statement*
of it. They feel like they get points for having gray hair, a kind of
moral superiority." I felt a little busted. Pretending you're younger
than you are is one form of vanity, but ostentatious authenticity,
when it becomes too preening and holier-than-thou, can be a
different kind of vanity—and the latter kind, Nora thinks, is a
"luxury" of youth. "People start coloring their hair before the end
of the story," Nora said, meaning before the end of actual youth.
"In their thirties they're frightened of turning into visions of their
mother. The big difference between our mothers and us is *only*
chemical. When my mother was my age, you could have two
colors of hair—blue or pink. Pink was called strawberry blond."
Nora, who's sixty-six, has no plans to stop coloring her hair.

A lot of my friends looked at me with the same incredulity
that I might have looked at them with had they told me that they
were going to get breast implants or run off with the electrician.
I wasn't talking about any big deal here, really—I mean, it's just
hair—but I realized that the gulf between the two camps, the
embracers and the resisters, is pretty vast.

But of course the subject isn't really *just* hair. As little kids we are encouraged by the toy manufacturers to engage in "hair play." Companies such as Mattel spend zillions of dollars and hours studying how kids actually play, what they call their play "patterns," and for girls, playing with hair—their dolls' or their own—is right at the top of the heap for how they like to spend their time. <u>Playing with hair supposedly taps into our most basic maternal and social instincts.</u> The apotheosis is a product Mattel sells called Fashion Fever Grow 'N Style Styling Head. It's just an oversize Barbie head, no torso, with hair that "grows" so you can spend hours styling it.

Hair is the salient shorthand sign we use to communicate to others who we want them to think we are. We can try on different personas and adjust it daily—one day ironed straight, the next waved; another day done in a prim little chignon, the next a ruffled "bed head"; one day accessorized with teensy barrettes, the next with a knotted scarf. The variations are limitless, and none is permanent—a perfectly modern and perfectly American ideal. Hair is the ultimate fashion tool.

So why do I actually care what anyone does with her hair? Because at some point along the spectrum—from little girls pretending to be mommies, playing with their Barbies' hair, to a large majority of women over forty dyeing their own hair—we've lost a link with reality. The eight-year-old kid *knows* she's *playing,* but the dyed-blond sixty-year-old...not so much. The antiestablishment statements that certain styles of hair used to represent—long hair or Afros for men and women in the '60s,

Mohawks in the '70s and '80s, Day-Glo colors in the '90s—have become period pieces. Today it seems as if the most provocatively political statement a woman can make with her hair is to let it be naturally gray.

There is, I think, the beginning of a breach in the culture that reminds me of the contentious, visceral divisions between women who work for pay and those who stay home with their children. I found a sort of proud, "we-know-better-than-you-weak-ninnies" sanctimony among the gray-haired true believers, and a proud, "how-dare-you-judge-my-choices-because-I-do-this-for-myself-to-feel-good-about-*me*" defensiveness in the committed-to-dyeing camp.

WHEN I MADE MY DECISION to go gray, I had no idea that the choice would elicit such emotionally laden responses. I decided to expand and even sort of formalize my "advisory board" of friends—more of a focus group than a support group. They ranged in age from their midthirties to midsixties and ran the gamut of professions—psychologists, designers, writers, home-makers, volunteers, marketers, and entrepreneurs. Of the fifteen, three had gray or white hair.

As I convened our first lunch, I worried that the women would find the topic absurdly unimportant, and given our busy lives, the time stolen from their days might be an intrusive sacrifice.

I couldn't have been more wrong.

Everyone seemed delighted to have a serious pretext to talk

thoughtfully for a couple of hours about almost nothing *but* hair. The conversations were lively. And revelatory.

Rachel, a fifty-four-year-old daughter of socialist parents who also happens to be a shrink with long, curly, darkly dyed hair, spoke of her sense of guilt about dyeing her hair because she felt as if she had sold out the antiplastic values of her Woodstock Nation youth. She sounded almost panicky when she confessed that in the middle of caring for her cancer-ridden mother, she still worried about getting her roots touched up. Were her priorities all screwed up?

Before Rachel finished speaking, Emily, the midforties founder of her own design studio (whose hair is long, wavy, and dyed), sought to alleviate Rachel's guilt. She positively glowed when describing how her time at the hair salon was her only private time during the month, away from screaming babies and work demands and spousal interaction. It was the one moment when she felt pampered and free to just think.

"So do any of you pluck your gray hairs?" asked Sara, a midforties magazine editor with naturally brown shoulder-length hair. Sara was genuinely interested in whether other people plucked and if the plucking might have any long-term negative consequences. "I'm fundamentally cheap and refuse to buy into the 'color racket,' but I want to postpone the gray as long as possible," she said. I silently thought that the endgame of the plucking strategy didn't seem like a very good outcome to me; bald patches look a lot worse than gray hair.

A chic fortysomething editor confessed that at thirty-five,

when her hair was first turning gray, a colleague remarked, "You look so distinguished!" As she told our group, "That comment was *so* not working for me." Neither was her husband's crack that when she dyed her own hair at home, she looked like Elvis Presley.

The two therapists in the group, both of whom color their hair, said they found that if they modified their looks too drastically, it upset their patients. Superficial consistency in a shrink, it turns out, is a desirable thing. And for them it served as a virtuous, feel-good reason — *It's about professionalism and sensitivity to others' needs, not personal vanity* — to keep coloring.

Each woman talked about how it simply made her feel good about herself to take care of her hair — and by that, most of them meant dyeing their hair.

At first the "uncolored" women were mainly silent on the sidelines as the other women spoke. Monique, a former fashion editor and now, in her sixties, a garden designer, was the one woman at the lunch with perfect white hair. Naturally shy, she said, "It never occurred to me to dye," when I asked her. Monique went gray very young, and I think that her hair became a sort of logo — a powerful differentiating tool in the competitive world of fashion. She did mention that cabdrivers often shouted out to her while she walked along the street, "Great hair, lady!" And had I polled my fifteen friends that day, I think to a woman we would have agreed that Monique had the best hair at the table.

Betsy, a fifty-one-year-old porcelain artist and former hat

designer with chin-length graying hair, said that she was wrestling with the whole "lowlights" concept of reverse coloring, adding dark streaks to her gray. If you search "gray hair" on the Internet, a lot of the information you'll discover covers exactly how women can add "dimension" to their hair by introducing a variety of colors. I personally think this is simply one more way the beauty industry tries to keep us on their regimens. But "lowlights" might effectively change the subject from age-versus-youth truthfulness to plain-versus-stylish aesthetics.

The fifty-two-year-old writer Kit, who highlights her brown hair, took me aside after the luncheon. She was clearly fired up. "I thought the discussion today was riveting," she said. "Such difficult and complicated stuff. One thing that struck me was the repeated clash between guilt over vanity and doing things to oneself for oneself. So the feminist vies with the moralist/purist; the wise hippie who wants to do things naturally debates with the shrewd, take-charge inner businesswoman who believes in taking action. As always, we are at cross-purposes because we feel both things; we are both things. The puritanical voice says we are being deceptive if we do things to hide our age; the pragmatic voice says we are simply taking things into our own hands, that age is a relative thing. I guess what is important is that we know ourselves well enough to know *why* we are doing things, when they have meaning and when they don't, and what the costs are to the rest of our lives."

I was fascinated and, frankly, surprised by the powerful reactions of so many of the people with whom I talked as I started going "natural." It was as if a lightbulb went off over everyone's head: we *sort of* know on some subliminal level that most of us are faking it—these days, a majority of American women over forty dye their hair—but we seldom actually let ourselves *think* about this and what it implies.

By looking at and talking about this one nearly universal focus of intense vanity, I realized I'd poked into the center of a great collective anxiety. Today it is the ubiquity of dyed hair, more than any other single thing, that allows women (and many men) to conjure the kind of person they want to appear to be.

All of my conversations early on in my own process of going gray convinced me more than ever that this apparently trivial subject was, in fact, absolutely nontrivial to the psyches and identities and lives of women.

I WANTED TO SEE WHAT the experts had to say about authentic aging. I hoovered up the relevant literature at my neighborhood bookstore. I discovered books by the bagful on different ways I could maintain a youthful appearance, looking fortyish until I died (which made me imagine how the *"ish"* would become *"yeesh"* around seventy) by disguising the realities of gray hair, wrinkles, and loss of muscle tone. Or books that, at best, passingly asserted the *fabulousness!* of gray. None of the information was fresh: just as we all know we should not smoke, should be moderate in our intake of food and drink, and should exercise and avoid harsh lighting, we also know that surgery can make flesh smoother, tighter, and plumper (with the important exception of the flesh of the neck, as Nora Ephron hilariously explained in her book).

There were serious books about aging, too, from George Vaillant's seminal academic analysis of how different people grow older differently *(Aging Well)*; to the works of polemicists such as Betty Friedan *(The Fountain of Age)*, Germaine Greer *(The Change: Women, Aging, and the Menopause)*, Simone de Beauvoir *(The Coming of Age)*, and Carolyn Heilbrun *(The Last Gift of Time: Life Beyond Sixty)*, reaffirming the status of older women; to the writings of journalists such as Peggy Orenstein and Letty Pogrebin, centering around women in their fifties; to the offerings of (young, pretty) Naomi Wolff, looking critically at our cultural norms of beauty. A few brave writers, such as the late M. F. K. Fisher or Colette, used fiction to explore the fear and sense of loss that most women feel as they approach menopause. There were a few books that looked at how to care for gray hair and how to dress and apply makeup for a new color palette, but these glossed over, or more often entirely ignored, the stigmas, spoken and unspoken, attached to gray hair.

And while I benefited from reading all of these books, the more I read, the more I found myself becoming dispirited. A simple, too willfully PC "you're-not-getting-older-you're-getting-*better*" mantra simmered within all of the so-called second-adulthood books. The tone tended toward strenuous cheerleading, and I was not a bit inspired by exhortations about embracing my "inner goddess" and how cool being a "crone" could be. (Frankly the very word "crone" horrified me.) The options offered seemed to buy into the extreme either-or cultural stereotypes — a woman has two choices as she ages: turn herself into some freakish Joan Collins / Faye Dunaway wannabe or else become a let-it-all-hang-out hippie. And the tendency of many of the books toward "spiritual" mumbo jumbo made even New Agey me want to run screaming in the opposite direction.

None of them was the clear-eyed, plainspoken, practical guidebook that I wanted to help me figure out what it meant to navigate my middle age a bit more confidently, with a little less fakery and fuss.

I discovered, in short, that I was really going to have to figure out going gray on my own.

It was time to see what my family thought. My husband, Kurt, is a paradox. On the one hand, as a novelist and essayist, he demands highly nuanced precision of thought, and sloppy thinking is *not* something he suffers quietly. Yet on the other hand, he frequently hasn't noticed changes in my hair that I considered major — with the notable exception of the time in my midthirties when I got my hair cut extremely short and he remarked, deflatingly, that I now looked like a "lady golfer." It's not that he's oblivious to his surroundings; it's just that I sometimes think he operates on a more cerebral than physical plane. So his "Sure, why not?" response to my telling him that I was going to let my hair go gray was pretty much what I had anticipated.

And his laissez-faire, I'm-game-for-anything approach to most things has been a huge and liberating advantage for me — freeing me to start and quit jobs with the assurance of his backing or travel to places such as Hanoi and Mumbai and Kilimanjaro on a whim. Most important, regarding this latest decision, he had been supportive — or at least silently accepting — during the twenty-odd years that my hair went through its zigzag morphings of color. Because we had been together since we were practically children — losing parents, changing jobs, raising children, starting businesses, dealing with illness — I hopefully believed that our relationship and whether he found me sexy didn't hinge on the color of my hair.

But... who knew? *His* hair was still mostly *not* gray. And his late mother had short gray Gertrude Steinish hair for the twenty-five years I knew her. Although I adored her, I worried now that I might end up reminding him of her, and that thought sent chills up my spine.

My older daughter, Kate, was supportive. But of course she would be. At ten she became enthralled with Japanese animation and comics — ones in which most of the characters had neon, never-seen-in-nature-on-this-planet hair colors. At twelve, emulating her anime heroes and playing with burgeoning notions of her own identity, she started dyeing large chunks of her own hair shades of pink, turquoise, and green. I thought it was glorious. And why wouldn't I? She wasn't tattooing butterflies on her neck or piercing her tongue. Each stage of the rainbow stripes looked radiant in her blond hair—I particularly liked how the blue faded to a trace of copper wash at the tips as it grew out. So what would be so weird about some gray in Mom's hair? She'd told me that some of her friends thought that with my dark hair, I resembled Trinity, the female character in *The Matrix,* and I found that comparison flattering and cool, but I took heart from the fact that lots of characters in Japanese animation had dramatically *white* hair. Maybe my natural look would be sort of, kind of, maybe…hip.

As for encouragement from my younger daughter, Lucy, in eighth grade at the time and the most bracingly frank person in the family…not so much. "Oh, God, no," she said. "*Please* keep dyeing your hair. I don't want to have one of the *old* mommies at school."

And although I knew she was *sort of* kidding, Lucy's comment rattled me. I was a little surprised by her fervor. If anything, given her natural candor, I assumed that she would have embraced a more visually candid me. I also realized that what she was really worried about was that, by looking different from the other moms (not a single other mom in her grade had gray hair), I'd draw attention to us. We'd be *different.* And when you're thirteen, different isn't such a good thing. And deep down I knew that she, like my friends who'd cautioned me not to stop dyeing, was right—in some sense I undoubtedly *would* appear older.

But since I'd already made up my mind, damn it, I had resisted considering that uncomfortable truth. With the reddish-brown hair of my late forties, I didn't really think I actually looked younger than I was. But the dye job at least confused the issue, changed the subject. Letting my hair become its natural color would be an unmuddling of the age issue, a definitive announcement to the world that *I'm no longer young.*

Contemplating what I was about to do, I discovered that I couldn't just order the fear to stop bubbling up. My fiftieth birthday, after all, was just a year away. I began to have sleepless nights, obsessing over the end of my youth. But why? I mean, get real — *it's only hair.* I have never made a career out of my looks, although I've always tried to make the most of them — and perhaps that's what was scary: that I'd look like I *just didn't care anymore,* that I had decided to *let myself go.*

Through most of my professional life, I had worked mainly in corporate environments, most recently as the worldwide creative director of Nickelodeon, the cable TV channel and media brand for kids. That job demanded that I look young enough to credibly appear to know what the tween viewers of the channel might be obsessing about and yet also old enough to effectively manage dozens of twentysomething employees. But now, at forty-nine, I had removed myself from that version of the corporate world, with those implicit expectations of youthful cred.

So what was the big deal? Did I really think that overnight I'd turn into Barbara Bush or Queen Elizabeth? And *because* of my fears, I decided that giving up artificial hair color was exactly the right thing for me to do. I've always hated being told by anyone the choices I *must* make and the ways I *must* act, and I realized that most of my anxieties about letting my hair go natural were driven, not to put too fine a point on it, by a media-induced cultural hysteria that gray equals desiccated, unsexy, over. I was about to find out what it felt like to swim against the tide.

Only Her Hairdresser Knows for Sure

IN 1950, when my mother was a young woman, fewer than 10 percent of American women colored their hair. Today, the estimates range from 40 percent to 75 percent for all adult women — and it follows that a solid majority of women over forty do so. Clairol's famous old advertising slogan — "Does she...or doesn't she?" — has lost its power and relevance. Any stigma and even any overt concession that artificial hair color amounts to a fib are quaint vestiges of another era. We've undergone a sea change. But how in the heck did we end up here?

Biologically, we as creatures are hardwired to seek the healthiest mates possible for procreation. Two of the most obvious markers for good health are clear skin and shiny hair, typically the provinces of youth. And aeons ago, when our female ancestors lived unimaginably hard lives and, in the main, probably died before reaching menopause, those external genetic signals were paramount. Compared to prehistoric times, ninety is the new forty. Since a woman's average life expectancy in the United States today is over eighty, and it's now easy for women to prevent pregnancy and perfectly possible for them to get pregnant in their forties and beyond, there is a disconnect between those ancient, superficial markers of genetic health and contemporary reality. Simply put, our minds and culture have not caught up evolutionarily. Well past their childbearing years, women still feel obliged to compete for male attention using those "must-make-as-many-healthy-babies-as-possible" standards of youthful hair and dewy skin—dyeing their hair the color it was in their (or someone's) prime childbearing years and chemically freezing their brows in the hope that they will continue to be desirable to strong, healthy creatures who can impregnate them.

Nonprocreative sex itself is genetically pretty pointless. Yet it constitutes 90-something percent of the sex that most of us have in our lives, and we enjoy it as much (or more) than the genetically meaningful kind. So trying to remain attractive past menopause is, evolutionarily speaking, just a...*habit* that we keep indulging.

The artificial-hair-color phenomenon is different, though, because as a mass cultural trend, it's very recent. Why, over just these last few decades, has what seems like a vestigial species memory—female gray hair = barren = unattractive—become more and more controlling?

Now that the oldest baby boomers are over sixty, and all seventy-seven million members of that culturally dominant generation are over forty, the disconnect will presumably become even more pronounced. For one thing, the forty million American women now in their forties and fifties are the largest number of females in the United States who have ever been in that age group at one time. That generation—mine—was the first to make "forever young" its permanent guiding principle. And there is no evidence that the younger generations are turning out differently in that respect—people in their thirties are no longer young, but they're at least as strenuously *youthful* as boomers were at that age.

And before we get to the late 1960s, we need to look back even further. Of course, colored hair has been intermittently fashionable for centuries, from Egyptian henna to the white-powdered wigs and hair of the 1700s. But a modern turning point—when artificial hair color was presented as up-to-date, democratic, the right thing to do—was at the Paris world's fair of 1867: hydrogen-peroxide hair bleaching was introduced alongside exhibits advocating changes in children's education and ways to improve the hygiene of the household. Then, after peroxide became available, patent hair colorings were introduced.

But it wasn't until the 1950s,—when the baby boomers were being born and big cosmetic marketers introduced easy, non-peroxide-based dyes for home use, advertising them on the new mass medium, television—that American women began to dye their hair en masse. Until then, women who colored their hair were widely considered harloty adventurers—the Mae Wests and Jean Harlows and tens of thousands of local, uncelebrated town-trampy versions. But suddenly, in the '50s, the great new age of artificiality (plastics! Dacron! Naugahyde!) and better living through chemistry, any woman could begin to experiment with her image more subtly and secretly, in the privacy of her home and with little risk of the permanent damage that earlier processes entailed.

In the 1957 beauty section of *Good Housekeeping*, the "Be Good to Your Hair" feature mentions newfangled "color rinses." In 1959 the magazine ran an article called "Hair Coloring: Is It for You?" "Hair coloring is a changed subject nowadays. Subtle rinses and mild formulas for lighting blond hair can be just about as safe (and about as controversial!) as most other cosmetics. Now *permanent* coloring—tempered by discretion and scrupulous

precautions—has an accepted role, too." The two-thousand-word primer goes into minute detail about this new business of coloring your hair at home.

Back then, before artificially colored hair had become ubiquitous, marketers were still obliged to acknowledge with a smirk the little lie they were enabling. Clairol's "Does she...or doesn't she?" advertising campaign started making it more generally acceptable and desirable for respectable women to color their hair.

One 1969 execution of the campaign featured a young mother playing in the snow with her twin toddlers, and the plausible-deniability tagline "Hair color so natural only her hairdresser knows for sure!" "Everything's more fun, more exciting when she's around. Her quick laugh, her bright good looks, even the color of her hair, so fresh and shining. Like a kid's."

"Artificial color from a box—but so fresh and natural." The

push by Clairol and its competitors to make dyed hair *normal* was going full bore during the '60s, just as let-it-all-hang-out honesty and "naturalness" were becoming cardinal virtues and modern mass feminism was starting to emerge. It was a contradiction, and one that the marketers addressed directly—and then encouraged us girls and women to finesse and fudge and forget.

A 1975 Clairol ad for Loving Care ran with a tiny image of a young woman giving the peace sign—this is the year the Vietnam War finally ended—and the following copy:

> They put a man on the moon. Why can't they cover my gray without changing my natural haircolor?
>
> I don't want to be cantankerous. But *naturalness* is a big thing with me. In people and food and especially my looks. Unfortunately, my gray hair is also natural. And mine is really getting me down because it makes me look older than I feel.
>
> But become a bleached blonde? Or a peroxide brunette? It's just not my style. Because no matter how natural-looking the color turned out, it would be somebody else's natural, not mine....
>
> Loving Care...has no peroxide. It just covers up the gray without changing your natural color....
>
> Beautiful. Now that I use Loving Care, you can't see any of my grays. I've got my natural color with some nice highlights I haven't seen since I was a kid....
>
> Now, if they would just put a woman on the moon.

By the end of the decade, the idea that all women *needed* to improve their lives by means of hair color was overt. The marketing messages concerning hair color had shifted from cheerful, slightly tentative encouragement to don't-be-a-prig, jump-on-the-bandwagon zeal. "I didn't believe haircoloring was for me," says the pseudotestimonial copy in a 1979 ad for Miss Clairol. "*Now* I can't believe I waited....I had some pretty strange notions about haircoloring. I was afraid it would be too 'obvious.' I was sure it wouldn't look natural. But now that I did it, I feel prettier. Younger. Even a little sexier. And I can't imagine why I waited so long."

"*Younger. Sexier.*" The ongoing implications of the 1960s youthquake—of being inculcated with sensibilities defined by

rock and roll and sexual freedom and a kind of do-your-own-thing relativism about life in general—were various and contradictory. Even when we were young and absolutely sure of right and wrong, passionately furious at war and injustice and establishment phoniness, we also cared desperately about how we looked, from our footwear (sandals? Earth Shoes? Frye boots?), to our Indian dresses and bell-bottom jeans, to our tie-dyed T-shirts and Guatemalan guayaberas, to—especially—our luxuriant *hair*.

Today, three and four decades after the baby boomers' countercultural transformation of the culture, we have held on to the hedonistic forever-young part of our Woodstock dreams much more tenaciously than the open-and-honest-and-authentic part. Yes, women really have come a long way toward equality of opportunity and social empowerment. Yet at the same time there has been a *narrowing* of the range of acceptable looks for women. Women may now be CEOs and TV news anchors, and openly indulge their sexual appetites—but only if they appear eternally youthful. And a main requirement is a hair color other than gray or white.

Our present era of mainstreamed artificial hair color began in the 1950s and '60s. But the tipping point came, I believe, during the 1980s—when the oldest baby boomers entered middle age and the grand illusion of permanent physical youthfulness really became widespread and almost obligatory. I don't think it's a coincidence that Ronald Reagan, a man with impossibly black hair in his seventies (as well as glowing, ruddy skin), blithely and belovedly presided over the country during that decade.

And now the 24-7 media culture that has arisen since then thrusts forever-young famous people in our faces constantly. The fantasy—sold by every women's magazine, every celebrity magazine, every TV program—is that any of us can aspire to look like Diane Sawyer at sixty-two or Goldie Hawn at sixty-two or Sophia Loren at seventy-three. And most of us start believing that delusion on some level, even if, in *US Weekly* or on Web sites such as AwfulPlasticSurgery.com, we occasionally glimpse Goldie Hawn or Mary Tyler Moore in real life looking like the sixty-two- or seventy-year-old grandmothers they are.

When even Oprah Winfrey has episodes of her TV show devoted to extreme makeovers (including the transformation of Coretta Scott King not long before her death), we know that the desire to look as young as possible is permanently entrenched in our culture. On an *Oprah* show last year about "aging brilliantly" and "embracing the age you're in," the seventy-one-year-old actress Diahann Carroll said, "There's no reason to be gray-haired." In *I Feel Bad About My Neck,* Nora Ephron wrote, "There's a reason why forty, fifty, and sixty don't look the way they used to, and it's not because of feminism, or better living through exercise. It's because of hair dye." During a recent segment on the *Today* show, a hair adviser told the audience—a plurality of whom were middle-aged and female—that a woman over forty "should never show her gray," period, and that women over fifty should have a "multidimensional" artificial color.

This fudging of the truth has been further reinforced by media technologies. At a dinner party not long ago, I sat next to a lighting director for one of the late-night network talk shows and was surprised to learn from him the degree to which people on live television are "enhanced" to look younger—or, anyway, less obviously old. I knew that clever lighting, expert makeup, and the Barbara Walters "softening" effect (where Vaseline is smeared on a camera lens to blur the wrinkles and bags) were all tools of the trade. But I had no idea that there was a new electronic version of lens oiling. This feature, which won a technical Emmy, fuzzes detail exclusively in the flesh-tone-colored parts of the video image, while the remainder of the picture retains full detail. The result is that faces look smoother, younger. As high-definition television becomes widely adopted, exposing every pore and imperfection, the demand for such digital fibbing will only increase. (And indeed, some on-air talent have contractual agreements that their programs will *not* be broadcast in high definition precisely because they feel they will look too "real.") It's real-time live-action Photoshop. And none of us at home are the wiser. It's literally impossible for us to measure up to the preternaturally youthful faces we see on TV or in magazines.

It's a given that every visible pore, wrinkle, splotch, sag, and bag will be airbrushed from the photographs of celebrities in magazines. Only when it was revealed last year that someone in the CBS publicity machine photoshopped twenty excess pounds off the first solo female evening news anchor were (minor, passing) ethical questions about truth and illusion raised—as if this very thing hadn't been done before with male anchors, and as if TV news talent are supposed to be the last guardians of visual truth. Uh, has anyone checked out the artificially enhanced hair of Chris Matthews (sixty-one) or Tim Russert (fifty-seven) or Lou Dobbs (sixty-one) or John McLaughlin (eighty) lately? I could go on. And on.

Katie Couric was rightfully upset by someone altering her image without her permission—but come on, it's just a matter of degree, since there's nothing natural about her hair color. The hapless CBS PR department just did what they always do—make everyone look better than they do in real life. It was just that in Couric's instance, the form didn't fit the function, since at that moment gravitas and truth telling were the brand attributes at hand. Meanwhile, the people *watching* her can now accomplish the same thing with themselves at home: Hewlett-Packard offers a new "slimming" feature on still cameras that automatically makes people appear thinner.

I think that all this social and cultural pressure, subtle but ferocious, to cosmetically keep up with the Joneses — especially when the Joneses in question are of the Catherine Zeta variety — shapes more of our personal choices than ever before. Those comparisons are inevitable — we're all human — but they don't need to tyrannize or paralyze. Isn't individualism a core American value? "Most of us want to fit in with our peers, but we don't want to fit in too well," the psychologist Daniel Gilbert wrote last year in his bestseller *Stumbling on Happiness*. "We prize our unique identities, and research shows that when people are made to feel too similar to others, their moods quickly sour and they try to distance and distinguish themselves in a variety of ways." So when we try too hard to look like everyone else, we are probably doing the *opposite* of what would make us happy. And having an obsession with a certain narrowcast version of physical youthfulness is a surefire way to create false expectations that end up making us miserable. Just because we have the same hair color as Jennifer Aniston or Julianne Moore, or drive the same car as Cameron Diaz, or wear the same dress as Eva Longoria or Mischa Barton, doesn't mean our lives will in any way resemble theirs. "As bald men with cheap hairpieces always seem to forget," Gilbert wrote, "acting as though you have something and actually having it are not the same thing, and anyone who looks closely can tell the difference." If you substituted "gray-haired women" for "bald men," and "dye jobs" for "cheap hairpieces," you had me for most of my adult life. As I discovered, my jet-black fortieth-birthday transformation didn't magically turn me into the new Madonna.

Maybe the same is true for you.

As a generation, we baby boomers have aerobicized, Botoxed, and hair dyed our way into a collective denial of the fact that we are getting old. We all sort of know that we're not *really* fooling anyone, but we can't let go of the wishful illusion.

I talked about this with Anna Quindlen, the commentator and novelist. "All of us want to believe that we don't look our age," she said, "and people our age have absorbed this message that diet, exercise, and doing the right thing will let you live forever." Anna is fifty-five. "We're the first generation who covertly" — that is, not literally but as a form of magical thinking, as in the way children see things — "believes that we're not going to die. And that profoundly influences our approach to aging."

And the business of keeping us boomers young-looking is big. The "cosmeceutical" market — skin products with both cosmetic and medicinal components — accounted for $13.3 billion in sales last year. That's up from $2.6 billion just five years ago. And now that Avon's 2005 Global Women's Survey revealed that 80 percent of American girls and women between *fifteen and twenty-four* believe that they already show unattractive signs of aging, it's an absolute guarantee that the market is only going to get larger and larger. If adolescents are worried about aging, boomers should just give it up.

In one survey of eight hundred women, 87 percent said their hair was a "part of their personality," and 58 percent said their hair, for better or worse, strongly affected their confidence. Because of our particular, emotionally laden regard for hair, the hair-care market is a large, high-growth part of the beauty industry. In the same survey, when respondents were asked to report the color of their hair, "gray" was not even an available option.

As a rough guide, 50 percent of people will have 50 percent gray hair by age fifty—which translates into a huge market. Some hair-color marketers estimate, hopefully, that as many as three-quarters of women color their hair, although some research puts the number closer to half that, including women in their teens, twenties, and thirties. But we all know plenty of neighborhoods—maybe we live in one—where the percentage is easily 75 percent or closer to 100 percent. According to a piece last year in *Washingtonian* magazine, "three-quarters of [white] Washington women color their hair."

UNTIL I STOPPED COLORING my hair, I'd never dared to calculate what it was costing me. When I did the calculations, my mind boggled. Because I so hated the sight of gray roots, I went to the hairdresser, on average, once every three weeks between ages twenty-five and forty-nine. Every three weeks for twenty-four years added up to a total expenditure, not adjusted for inflation, of $65,000. Staggering. I asked my investment adviser what the sum, had I invested it, would be worth today. "Three hundred thousand dollars," he told me. In other words, I could have paid for both my daughters' private college educations out of my hair-color-budget line—if I had had a hair-color-budget line. Yet even during times when cash was tight, after I quit my Nickelodeon job in 1996, it never occurred to me to give up my hair maintenance—good color was essential, nonnegotiable. It allowed me to feel groomed and competent and with-it.

Multiply me times millions of women—including many, it's true, who spend only hundreds a year compared to my several thousand, but also including others who spend much more—and you see why hair color is such big business. Hair care was the largest growth segment of the personal-care market during the 1990s, driven largely by the middle-aged baby-boomer population.

And hair color is a dazzlingly fabricated business of fabrication. Just as a taste, here are the colors—that is, *some* of the colors—sold by just one company, L'Oréal: Cool Blonde, Copper Blast, Red Copper Spritz, Iced Coffee, Hot Mahogany, Lively Auburn, Red Pulse, Funky Cherry, Chilled Plum, Electric Black, Chardonnay, Sunset, Auburn Dream, Wheat, Palomino, Amber, Mocha, Caramel, Teak, Redwood, Plum Oasis, Cocoa, Walnut, Tawny, Caution Red, Ebony, Espresso, Chestnut, Biscotti, Vanilla Icing, Platinum Crystal, Starlet, Pure Diamond, Blush Blonde, Candle Glow, Champagne Cocktail, Blonde Chiffon, Caramel Kiss, Shimmering Sands, Flaming Red, Ruby Rush, Blowout Burgundy, Sunset Blaze, Copper Shimmer, Cardinal,

Ruby Fusion, Brilliant Bordeaux, Cinnamon, Dark Amethyst, Crushed Garnet, Chocolate Cherry, Midnight Ruby, Downtown Brown, Crème Brûlée, Sparkling Amber, Hot Toffee, Bronze Shimmer, Havana Brown, French Roast, Starry Night, and Black Leather. (*Black Leather?* For the life of me I cannot figure why *anyone* would want his or her hair to look like black leather.) Nowhere among them are, say, "Radiant Granite" and "Silver Steel" and "Alpine Glacier." Romantic fantasies about gray and white hair are not encouraged—there's just not much money in it.

Hello? *Your Roots Are* Really *Showing* — *My Bad Hair Year*

I'D MADE MY DECISION to let my hair go gray, but that didn't mean I was brave enough simply to stop coloring and go cold turkey. I'd watched my good friend, the novelist Susanna Moore, do precisely that. She'd quit her dark-brown dye jobs when they simply became more of a hassle than they were worth. Susanna, almost six feet tall and a former model and occasional actress, has a highly individualistic, almost theatrical style. On a day when she feels she looks her worst, heads turn when she walks into a restaurant or down the street. She has a kind of presence that I would love to have but that in a million years I could never pull off. Characteristically, rather than cut her long hair to minimize the unsightliness of her roots growing in, Susanna instead chose to amplify her transitional phase with a flamboyant gesture, adding a dramatic reverse–Susan Sontag streak of black into her whitening hair. She performed a magician's sleight of hand by drawing attention to her shocking black streak and away from her roots. It was a bravado stroke and quite successful. Imagine a beautiful, whimsical Cruella De Vil.

I like to think I have a pretty distinctive personal style, but it's nothing like Susanna's. At 5'3", I find that my look tends toward the quietly severe—traditional silhouettes, *never* a plunging neckline or flounce, minimal jewelry, little adornment. More Audrey Hepburn than Audrey Tatou. More architect than artist. My one deviation from austerity has been my creative use of hair color.

Watching Susanna let her gray grow in in such a visible way helped me think about how I actually wanted to *feel* as my hair grew out. And thinking about that forced me to acknowledge that while I was happy to be quitting artificial color, I wanted the transition to be as invisible as possible to others. I realized that I was not comfortable drawing too much attention to myself and never had been. I have never thought of my looks as anything other than regular, relying instead on my competence or humor for my self-esteem. But at the same time, like most of us, I wanted other people to find me physically appealing. I knew that having a giant white skunk streak down my scalp as my hair grew out wasn't going to make me feel good. I was more timid than that. And since I'd always been identified with long hair, I was vain enough to refuse to cut it. So I had a problem. How exactly does a person who's timid yet concerned about her looks handle letting dark dye grow out? Aside from Susanna, I'd not observed anyone else doing it.

I worked with my colorist, Inge Pumberger, to manage the transition. In my wishful thinking, I'd assumed that I could just strip the color out. Inge convinced me that stripping would be a disaster, nearly impossible—each inch of my hair had absorbed different degrees of tint each time I'd put in the single-process color, so the end result of stripping would have been a ghastly, horizontally striped, porcupine-quill effect. So to minimize the thickening band of gray that was growing in near my scalp, Inge put in blond highlights that blended with the gray roots as they grew. And then she put a toner over the whole thing to blur the edges between the grays and blonds even more. I began to fully appreciate just how tricky going gray was going to be.

I wasn't so sure about this transitional strategy—I felt as if I looked like I was trying to go blond, not white, but I trusted Inge to know what she was doing. I had been addicted to color for a quarter-century, and if I needed the colorist's version of Nicorette or methadone to help liberate me, so be it.

As one of my tell-as-many-people-as-you-can-so-you-won't-back-out strategies, I offered to write about my experience for *More* magazine and to be photographed during the various stages of decolorization. When I made the proposal, I imagined photographers and stylists pampering me, treating me like "talent." I actually fantasized that I might be "discovered" through this lark; okay, I was way too old and the wrong gender to become a late-starting Beatle, maybe, but perhaps I could get a gig as a white-haired model in ads touting cruise ships or fractional-ownership jets.... In fact, the first shoot, when my hair had no discernible roots, was relatively fun.

The second shoot proved to be less fun. The anticipatory modeling fantasy had evaporated. My gray roots were visible around my ears and beneath the top layer of hair. This posed a serious challenge to the makeup artist—a 6'2" twentysomething Ethiopian and actual former fashion model—who decided that the best way to reveal for the camera what minimal gray I had was to slick back my hair with a heavy-duty goo that smelled like shoe polish. I hated my greasy hair but felt too insecure to suggest we should try something different. My product-infused hair made me look like a cheesy "before" model in some late-night infomercial.

I've never worn much makeup. I had had makeup professionally applied once before, for a corporate photo in the '90s, and hadn't much liked that experience—the heavy foundation and mascara, combined with my dyed hair, had made me look scary, like a younger Donatella Versace. With the best of intentions, my *More* makeup artist replicated that experience for me. The photographer's female assistant was an equally intimidating 6' former model—chic, skinny, and twenty-nine. (Hmmm, memo to magazine: when shooting "real" women, using former models at the shoot pretty much guarantees an anxious, self-loathing experience for the subject.) Happily, Hazel Hammond, the *More* photo editor, was fifty-one and in the process of letting her own hair go gray, so we felt an instant bond—but, like all the women in my vicinity that day, she was very tall, slim, and stylish. At 5' 3" and around 130 pounds, I felt like a troll. I was blindsided by how uncomfortable the experience made me feel. As I began my dive into authenticity, I was being professionally painted up—and felt authentic only in my dumpiness.

Hazel dressed me in a turquoise jewel-necked sweater, and since I was being shot only from the waist up, I wore my old baggy Levi's. As I sat for my first portrait, I felt the fifteen-pound tire around my waist spill over the top of my jeans, and as I tried to suck in my gut, hardly daring to breathe, my shoulders hunched and the snug sweater became sausage casing around every little pooch and sag in my body. Was there ever a more uncomfortable-seeming photo subject in the magazine's history?

Worse damage to my psyche was coming. I didn't need glasses until my forties and have never acclimated to them, wearing them only for driving and going to the movies. Until the photo shoot, I didn't understand that the wrinkle-free face I saw when I looked in the mirror without my glasses wasn't how I looked to everyone else: my mildly defective vision naturally airbrushed the blotches, bags, and wrinkles.

When Chris Fanning, the raffish young male photographer (whom I imagined spent the rest of his time photographing *Sports Illustrated* swimsuit models in Fiji rather than middle-aged housewives in Brooklyn), handed me test-shot Polaroids so I could see how I looked, I nearly burst into tears. The pictures showed a crinkly, age-spotted middle-aged face covered with not-so-fine perimenopausal hair. My new gray hair would be just *one* highly visible calling card announcing my over-the-hillness! Every single thing about me was old and unsexy.

When the glamorous makeup artist, innocently trying to calm my obvious anxiety, started talking about her gray pubic hair, I just wanted to squeeze my eyes shut and make everyone go away. It was all too absurd and vain and trivial, and discouraging. Surrounded by all of those very young, beautiful women and the handsome photographer, I *knew* what old felt like that day.

The struggle to reconcile my enthusiasm for the *principle* of becoming my authentic self with the dreary reality of my lengthening gray roots got worse. The toner my colorist chose to blend the root transitions turned my hair orangey, more reminiscent of Garfield the cat than Sarah Jessica Parker. The promotional self-encouragement did nothing to address how crummy my hair actually looked. In the first minute of social encounters, I developed a sort of Tourette's-like tic, talking about my "experiment" before anyone could comment. I was not just looking older but coming across as a little nutty.

The photograph on my driver's license is almost ten years old and shows me with long brown hair. Since 2001, before I even started going gray, whenever I've gone through airport security, I've felt compelled to make some jokey remark to the agents about how different I look from the ID picture. Returning from a trip to Washington, DC, early last year, I was required to show an Amtrak clerk a photo ID in order to buy a ticket. And for the first time since letting my hair go gray, I realized that my official identification image now truly looked nothing at all like me. When I showed my license to the Amtrak woman, she looked at it, looked at me, then looked back at the license. I knew I didn't appear to be a terrorist, but I didn't have any glib patter at the ready, so I sheepishly told the plain truth: "I know I don't look very much like my photo anymore—I quit dyeing my hair." I was totally embarrassed by the difference in my appearance, as if I were using a fake ID.

She smiled and shook her head when I babbled my hair-color confession. "Honey," she said, "I'm *never* going to quit dyeing my hair." The ticket clerk was a large African American woman with a neon stripe of purple sweeping off her right temple. I asked why she was so dedicated to dyeing her hair.

"Look, I'm fat, and with this purple stripe, people look at my hair and not my body. Besides, I've got a younger husband." *Aha.*

"If you don't mind my asking, how old are you?"

"Forty-two," she said.

"And how old is your husband?"

"Twenty-nine."

I'd gone to Washington for my book club (we were reading E. L. Doctorow's *The March* and decided to visit Gettysburg as a field trip), and I took the opportunity to interview hairdressers at George's Four Seasons, one of the salons that cater to DC's broadcast-news personalities and politicians.

"Most women," the owner's son and colleague, Sertac Ozturk, told me, "you can tell when they think they looked their best.

It's usually their late thirties—and nothing has changed for them since then, not their color, their cut, or their clothes." My frozen-in-time driver's license image was a reminder to me of how very recently I had been like the women he was describing.

Around the same time, during the first months after I'd quit dyeing, when I felt my hair looked particularly hideous, I had lunch with a fiftysomething male friend whom I hadn't seen in some time—and he told me that I looked like a movie star. You couldn't beat that feedback, but then again, because of the toner, I was actually ash-blondish at the time, so I'm not sure what he was really commenting on. But he gave me a precious glimmer of hope to think that my gray hair could still be attractive to men, at least men of a certain age.

Days later at the gym, I was shocked to discover that one of my role models, a lithe and formerly gray-haired midthirties trainer, had dyed her hair a dark chocolate brown. When I first decided to go gray, I had found her long silver hair inspirational but had never discussed it with her. Now I asked her about it. She told me she'd started to go gray at seventeen and had colored her hair just to have fun and play around with her image in her twenties, but at twenty-seven she'd decided to embrace the gray. "It was a wonderful experience. I called the grays 'my wisdom.' People always complemented me on my color—they thought I *dyed* it gray because I looked young."

So...why the backtracking *now?*

"I just got tired of looking old," she said with a shrug.

Ah, hell. If someone who had been that committed to her gray hair and who'd looked fabulous couldn't stick to it, what chance did I have?

I got more negative feedback at a party when a thirtysomething female friend remarked, "Oooh, how lovely—you're going gray just like a man!" I began to imagine that the women who told me they liked how the lighter hair color showed off my blue eyes were, behind my back, saying I looked old. The paranoia started to feed on itself.

I was even more bummed out by an experience I had with a well-known Manhattan entrepreneur and author friend in her midsixties, deeply sane and authentic. Early on in my process, she told me that, inspired by what I was doing, she was planning to let her artificially dark-brown hair go gray, too. What great support at such a crucial moment! When she confessed to me a couple of months later that her liberal-minded, white-haired husband and adult daughters had strongly argued against it, and that she'd backslid, deciding not to make the transition for now, I had firsthand experience of how very hard it was for women to resist the antigray bandwagon.

Three months into the process, when my hair was clearly coming in a mixed bag of minimal white and mostly steel gray, there was no doubt in my mind that I was actually looking older. I realized that when I'd started out I'd hoped my hair would instantly come in glistening white, not the salt-and-pebble effect that was actually happening. White to me was clean, fresh, and beautiful; gray, like rainy days, fog, and dirty laundry, was dreary, a downer. White was a color that women in their fifties didn't ordinarily have, so it would have felt almost like a new dye job rather than my natural hair. Gray was middle of the road, neither here nor there.

I asked my daughter Kate how she thought it was going. "Okay," she said. No, *really,* I insisted. "Well, with the blondish bits mixed in with the gray, it looks sort of like..." *What?* "Yellow teeth?" *Oh, my God. Yellow teeth?*

One night my husband and I and sixteen-year-old Lucy were late for our dinner reservation at a restaurant in Greenwich Village, and they went in first while I parked the car. When I arrived at the table, they were chuckling over what had just happened. The reservation had been for two, and the maître d' had evidently thought that non-gray-haired Kurt was out on a date with his very young blond girlfriend, and the waiter had even offered Lucy a glass of wine. They'd had to ask for a third chair to be brought to the table. "For my friend's mother, who'll be joining us," he had joked to the waiter. Ha ha ha.

I needed a fix from someone who had taken the plunge and who could urge me on. Ellen, a radiantly white-haired sixty-six-year-old friend, had started going gray in her forties. She told me that when she mentioned to her family twenty years ago that she might start dyeing her hair, her then ten-year-old son told her, "Don't do that, Mom—you'll be changing who you are." And so she didn't. I asked her what emotional meaning, if any, having white hair had for her.

"That I'm *different,*" she said, and I certainly knew what she meant — Ellen is well-to-do and lives on Manhattan's Upper East Side. "It's liberating. It's about loving myself for myself." She paraphrased Freud's notion of the id, ego, and superego by saying that we all have three faces: what we actually look like (our id), what we think we look like (our ego), and what we think others think we look like (our superego). For Ellen, living authentically is an exercise in trying to exist as little as possible in the realm where we are concerned about what we think others think we look like.

NOT LONG AFTER THAT LUNCH with Ellen, I found myself focusing *way* too much on what I thought others thought I looked like. My sense of physical and intellectual self-esteem was put on the line when my husband and I were to attend a dinner party with about thirty celebrated people. On the afternoon of the party, my older daughter and I, in a teen-mom bonding outing, had gone to a movie together. On the way home, I was bemoaning how much I disliked my hair and how my current cut seemed to make the in-between color look even worse. "Mom," Kate said, "it's simple — I can fix it for you." In the spirit of hope and trust and a sense that my almost-eighteen-year-old daughter was up to any challenge, I decided to let her trim my hair. The experiment started out swell, and I had one of the nicest just-us-girls experiences ever with her.

But as soon as I looked at her handiwork in the mirror, it became clear to me that there's a reason we pay professional hairdressers. (And, Joe, I hope you aren't reading this!) It is hard, really hard, to cut hair well. With the best of intentions, my daughter succeeded in creating a giant notch in the back of my hair. It wasn't quite Edward-Scissorhands-crazy-looking, but it was definitely weird. And I *had* to go to a fancy SoHo-loft soiree with a serious, change-the-world theme.

I went to the party knowing exactly one person aside from my husband and looking, in my mind, like Aunt Clara from *Bewitched*. I tried to keep my back to the wall and must have seemed awkwardly antisocial during cocktails. Once we all sat for dinner at a single long table, and the back of my head was no longer so visible, I relaxed — for a little while.

Then, to my horror, the host asked each of us to share with the group what we were most passionate about at the moment. I panicked as the others began to speak — thank God I was on the far side of the table from where they started! The first to go was Jacqueline Novogratz, the chief executive of the Acumen Fund, a global organization whose goal is to solve the problems of poverty. Jacqueline was passionate and articulate about a project that Acumen had developed to bring clean water to villages in Africa and India. Next up was Noah Feldman, the codirector of New York University's Center on Law and Security. I was familiar with Feldman's book *After Jihad: America and the Struggle for Islamic Democracy* and was thrilled to have the chance to listen to an insider talk about the situation in Iraq. My husband, damn him, was able to talk about the social and cultural revolutions of 1848 (central to the novel he was writing). Majora Carter, the urban activist and a 2005 MacArthur "genius" grant winner, described the work that her organization, Sustainable South Bronx, had initiated to bring sustainable development to the inner city. Her enthusiasm and vision were dazzling. Brian Greene of Columbia University, the leading string-theory theorist, riveted me with his discussion about the frontier of physics. Another MacArthur genius, the actress, playwright, and first Ford Foundation artist-in-residence Anna Deavere Smith, practically moved me to tears describing her work on a new one-woman play about death that she'd been researching. And so on. I had the great good fortune to be included at a gathering that could easily have been an answer to the question "If you could invite anybody in the world to a dinner party, who would it be?"

AND THEN, OH, GOD, it was my turn. I, the *only* nobody at the table, with my weird haircut, the guest who'd been acting sort of furtive, was terrified that my silly, self-centered explorations of aging and vanity would seem deeply unimportant, laughable. I mean, really. I wasn't solving international poverty or changing the way we see the world.

I had no choice but to speak, and I'm pretty shaky at public speaking under the best of circumstances, so you can imagine my fear to be following such accomplished people. I took the plunge and began to describe my "amateur social science" experiment with going gray. And amazingly, *blessedly,* almost everyone engaged in the topic. Maybe they were all simply too gracious not to appear interested. But after dinner three people approached me to talk further about the subject with genuine enthusiasm.

Several revelations emerged from that experience. First, my eccentric cut proved that no one really cares a whit about what anyone else's hair looks like. Second, and only somewhat contradictorily, even the most accomplished, serious people on the planet worry about aging *and* the way they look. And last, there are a lot of brilliant people out there who *are* tangibly making the world better. I went home inspired.

IN SOME WAYS letting my hair go gray was a bit like an intensive five-day-a-week-on-the-therapist's-couch crash course, but with no shrink to guide me. In August, halfway through the growing-in phase, the whole family went to Los Angeles to look at colleges for Kate. I found I couldn't bring myself to go for a swim at the chic Sunset Boulevard hotel where we were staying—the Chateau Marmont. It was just too intimidating for me to appear in a bathing suit and to have gray hair in LA, land of the preternaturally young and buffed and blond. There's no question I'd have been the *only* person at the Chateau Marmont pool—and maybe in a fifty-mile radius—with gray hair and freakishly white, untanned skin. Later, at a party, I met a recently divorced woman from Malibu who confessed that she had actually bucked convention and been gray in her twenties and thirties. She confided that after her divorce she had had to dye her hair. Her reasoning? Simple. "It's LA."

Throughout this bad-hair period, I wanted to shout, *Hey,*

everybody, I'm not any *different than I was six months ago—only my hair color has changed.* If white hair was something anyone *famous* had, apart from British actresses, Storm in the X-Men movies, and Meryl Streep in *The Devil Wears Prada,* then it wouldn't feel so weird—it'd just be another color to try on and live with. But in Southern California, I didn't see a single woman with gray hair during my entire stay. It seems that almost everyone who can afford it *really is* absolutely, professionally, unapologetically, committed to artificial youth—stereotypes and clichés can be true, can't they? I found my confidence faltering again.

I felt really down. And it's not like I hadn't tackled hard stuff before. I knew how tough it could be to make a real change in one's life. In 1993, after two over-the-top challenging years—both of my parents and my last grandparent died, my children were three and five, I had my big job at Nickelodeon, my husband was editing a weekly magazine—I realized that I was drinking too much. I was not drinking in a check-myself-into-rehab kind of way—I always accomplished what I had to do. But I was drinking in a way that numbed me to a degree that felt counterproductive and prevented me from fully appreciating the good things in my life. And I felt out of control. Through my own cobbled-together recovery program of willpower, yoga, acupuncture, and meditation, I stopped drinking. (For seven years. These days I allow myself to drink socially, very moderately, maybe once a week.)

While the choice to color my hair or not was a *wholly* different order of magnitude on the importance scale from rotting my liver or degrading my relations with the people I love, I realized that quitting booze and quitting hair color followed oddly similar paths: they both required me to face up to half-conscious fears and anxieties, to give up an easy and not unpleasant crutch, to reprogram habits, to accommodate myself to a new social identity, and to flout social pressure. Both forced me to spend time thinking seriously about how I wanted to live my life. If I wanted to be true to myself, which "me" was that supposed to be, exactly? Quitting hair color was the far more public act and provoked equally intense introspection. It wasn't harder than giving up wine, but it counterintuitively was much scarier.

Thank goodness that during my most discouraged time, I met Ann La Farge, a seventy-three-year-old book critic and former editor. Over tea one afternoon, she described her *aha!* moment of clarity when she decided to quit coloring her hair. At her fiftieth college reunion two years earlier, she had noticed that half the attendees were "got up" and the other half dressed for comfort. She realized that the ones who dressed for comfort were also nearly all the ones who didn't dye their hair—and that they overwhelmingly seemed to be having a better time than the other women. It was an instant realization for her that she'd far rather be among the "fun" half. She quit coloring cold turkey.

"I wasn't originally sure I was going to keep it that way. But then, after my hair grew in, one day my hairdresser was telling me he loved it. And as I was telling *him* that my friends said I looked older, a sixtyish man walked over from his chair in the salon and said, 'Mike Bloomberg here—and I think you look wonderful.'" Bloomberg, of course, is the mayor of New York City. La Farge went on to tell me about a Southern friend of hers who lectured Ann about her decision to go gray. The well-meaning woman urged her to keep coloring in no uncertain terms. "Everybody wants to look nice, Ann. I want to look my best. Why are you letting yourself *go?*"

This conversation made me wonder again at how choosing not to dye one's hair—and, increasingly, electing not to have plastic surgery—has become synonymous with "letting oneself go." Ann La Farge is the opposite of someone who has given up or stopped caring—she is slim, full of life, crackling with wit and warmth, a woman in her prime.

My family and I spent the last week that Summer of My Graying as geographically distant from Los Angeles as one can be in the United States, on Martha's Vineyard, Massachusetts. Archetypal LA and Martha's Vineyard residents share liberal political and cultural values, of course. People such as Bill and Hillary Clinton and even some Hollywood types spend a lot of time in both places. But there are striking differences—on the Vineyard, more of the women over fifty have gray hair than not. Even though the majority of the people on the island in August live elsewhere full-time, the overwhelming sense on the Vineyard is that fussing too strenuously with one's external, physical self is shallow, almost sinful. It seems as if the Puritanism of Massachusetts' founders still informs the upscale, Volvo-fied ethos of the place.

On a walk down the beach where we were staying, I did a

head count. More than six out of ten of the older women had gray hair—roughly the exact obverse of the national fraction of women who dye their hair. And then I saw one woman, on the small nudist section of the beach, easily sixty-five years old, with a flowing mane of pure white hair set off against her almost tropical, old-school dark tan. She was as close to a real-life Botticelli Venus as I'd ever seen.

Her beauty took my breath away, and I practically ran back to grab my husband so he could also see her. "Are you suggesting a threesome?" he joked. Unfortunately, before we could make it back to her spot, she had packed up and left for the day. I compared her smallish, naturally aging breasts and white hair with the pneumatically enhanced boobs and blond hair I'd seen on the women poolside at the Chateau in LA—and, for me, there was no contest. She radiated healthy beauty. That anonymous nudist immediately became one of my models for being attractive and old. I'm pretty sure I'll never have the courage to go nude in public—honesty and authenticity have their limits—but gray hair, that I can do.

Not long after the trip to Martha's Vineyard, I met Carmen Dell'Orefice. Carmen is today's only well-known white-haired model. She did her first cover shoot for *Vogue* in 1947 at age sixteen. She quit coloring her hair in 1973, at forty-two. "My third and last husband turned over to me one evening in bed. I thought he was going to caress my face—but instead he plucked out a white hair! I kept the hair and got rid of the husband."

Carmen seems to have wisdom. "The only lie that's a tragedy," she told me, "is the lie to oneself. It took me half my life to begin to know myself and the second half of my life to be true to what I know of myself—which is that I'm authentically screwy." Carmen staggered me with her energy and joie de vivre. On the day we spoke, she wore jeans, a crisp white shirt, little makeup, and her white hair pulled back into a ponytail. Carmen became another talismanic ideal—if only I could be half as self-aware as she at seventy-six, I would be a happy woman.

At the summer's end, ten months after swearing off dye, even I was getting more upbeat about the gray-haired me, but I was still just *becoming* gray, and my stylist, Joe, decided that I should grow out and lose my bangs, which I'd had since I was a teenager. He suggested I would look more glamorous without them, and I was all for glamour to mitigate the plainness of the gray. But the disappearance of the bangs also added a whole different level of hating-my-hair-ness to my life. At home I ended up clipping the new, longer front hair back with little bobby pins, which further emphasized the gray and made me look twelve going on sixty. The processed ends were so different from the new smooth gray growth that I finally couldn't take it anymore. I decided it was time to take drastic measures and cut serious inches off. I should have just done it at the beginning, but I wasn't entirely certain I could bear hating *both* my radical color *and* my radically new cut.

I had cut my hair short twice in my life. The first time was in my twenties, early in my marriage, and it had elicited my husband's unenthusiastic response. (To this day he insists that "looks like a lady golfer" wasn't code for "not so sexy," and to this day I don't buy it.) The second time, I was thirty-seven. As I mentioned earlier, in the space of six months, my father; mother; and last surviving grandparent, my mother's mother, had all died. My mother and her mother within the same twenty-four hours. It was beyond overwhelming. In some invented ritual informed by my loose study of Asian and Native American traditions, I decided to honor my family's deaths by cutting my hair. I needed to look really different—at least temporarily—because my life was really different, a kind of different that my old, trusted change-art tool of hair color couldn't fix.

After those two short-term, short-hair experiences, I was happy to find that *this* time, in the twenty-first century, I loved my new, shorter gray hair. It felt sleek and light and sophisticated, and reflected the way I was starting to feel about it—unencumbered and optimistic.

Finally, the feedback began to get more uniformly positive.

My husband professed to love the new style (except when I clipped my bangs back, or tucked my hair behind my ears).

In yoga class one day, a woman with whom I'd never spoken set her mat directly in front of mine, turned, and said, "Your hair looks fantastic. I've been watching as it's changed over the past few months, and you've given me the courage to think about quitting coloring my own hair." She made my day. Then, while I was waiting to meet one of my daughters outside a theater, a twentysomething guy stopped directly in front of me and said, "Hey, beautiful, what are you doing out here all by yourself?" Like all women who receive unwanted-yet-not-wholly-unflattering attention, I smiled at him dismissively as he walked past. He was a fairly unattractive guy, but he had passingly hit on old-lady *me*. *Not so bad*, I thought. Even the husband of my dyed-blond neighbor told me how much he liked my hair.

I also *loved* not being obliged to go to the salon every couple of weeks. I calculated: fifty or sixty new hours a year to read and see movies and plays, garden and ride a bike, or sit and talk with the people I love. And thousands of dollars saved.

My Mother, Myself, My Daughters—
How We Decide How We Want to Look

MOST OF THE WOMEN I talked to for this book admitted that their number one anxiety about letting their hair go gray was not a fear about how quickly they were closing in on their actuarial death dates—rather, it was that they'd instantly be seen as sexless, grandmotherly old ladies. How we rank ourselves in the looks and sexuality departments tends to get pretty firmly entrenched around puberty, so that's where I began my own introspective look back.

As children, my sister and I were required by our mother to dress exactly alike, until well into adolescence. It was weird. I have a black-and-white photograph of my sister and me when we were about seven and ten that was shot, strangely, with our backs turned to the camera, both wearing one of our identical Easter outfits—blond pigtails hanging straight down our backs, navy blue coats, white *Madeline*-style hats with ribbons between our braids, white gloves, white anklet socks, and black Mary Jane shoes. It looks like some spooky Diane Arbus image. It's clear to me now that how my sister and I *looked,* almost more than how we acted, was essential to our mother's social identity in upper-middle-class-aspiring-to-upper-class Kansas City.

As a child I internalized this notion that appearance was paramount — and specifically, a certain labor-intensive Midwestern-country-club presentation with perfect hair. My mother continued trying to exercise lifestyle control even after I was married by urging a wardrobe makeover on my husband, whose grays and blacks and navies and khakis she found too "drab." (Memo to TV producers: the scary-funny mother-in-law makeover reality-series concept is yours for the taking.)

My mother was pretty and always pulled together, high-strung, and more than a little Nancy Reagan–esque, even at home, even on weekends. I can count on one hand the number of times I ever saw my mother wash her own hair, and those occasions were as last resorts when we were on vacation and no one she knew would see her. Oddly, even while on vacation, I never noticed any gray roots — how she managed that is a complete mystery. Like other mothers of the time who invested a great deal of energy in their hair maintenance, when my mother went "swimming" the two times I remember her in a pool, she would breaststroke, straining her neck to keep her coifed hair out of the water. She had her hair done at least weekly, always following the styles of the time — the '60s bouffant look, transitioning to a more relaxed '80s pageboy. To protect those '60s hairdos, she'd sleep at night in a brushed-cotton cap very like the bootees that hospitals make you wear. As a member of that first generation of newly middle-aged women to whom Clairol was marketing hair color, my mother swallowed the idea hook, line, and sinker—she *always* had the same Elizabeth Taylor shade through her forties and fifties and sixties. Her mother dyed her hair a blondish-brown shade until her death at ninety-four. It never occurred to me at the time to ask my mother and grandmother why they didn't have gray hair—or even to consciously think about it.

So for me, growing up, dyed hair *equaled* femininity, and social acceptance hinged on looking no different than the people around us. Kind of a double whammy when it came time, thirty years later, to think about what it would mean to allow myself to reveal my natural gray hair. Abandoning artificial color was not only flouting New York City social norms but violating the very powerful female archetypes of my upbringing. Who would've thought—liberal contemporary New York and conservative Kansas City from an earlier era, totally in sync!

And while I've inherited a good deal of my mother's tightly wound nature, in contrast to her, I've been a freewheeling mother as far as appearances go. From the moment my daughters could button their own shirts and tie their shoes, I've let them throw together whatever kind of outfit they wanted. Crazy patterns with stripes? Sure, why not? In the service of expediency, I even allowed the kids, when they were little, to put on their school clothes at bedtime and sleep in them so that the morning routine would be easier. Who cares about a few wrinkles?

And I was equally relaxed when it came to hair. Kate, of course, applied her outrageous colors as an adolescent, and when Lucy was little, her hair was always charmingly disheveled. I actually took pride in the fact that both girls didn't have perfect hair all the time—to me, their undergroomed hair showed the world that they were self-confident, independent spirits with more important things on their minds. Today, after dabbling with highlights for a year or two, Lucy has naturally dark-blond, long hair and Kate adds blond highlights in her shoulder-length hair.

I clearly remember the rite-of-passage moment every mother of girls experiences—the moment I realized that my daughters were viewed inevitably as sexual beings. We were walking down a sunny street in SoHo one early summer day, both girls in their individually honed bohemian-chic outfits, and I in my jeans, Patagonia jacket, and rubber-soled Merrells. (And I digress, but comfortable shoes on women over forty are totally, not unlike gray hair, an "out of action" signifier.) And I realized that all of the male passersby were checking out my naturally blond thirteen- and fifteen-year-old daughters, not me. My hair was still dyed brown, so it wasn't *that* that put me lower on the horndog-browsing hierarchy. It was a subtle, happen-in-a-glance kind of transition, but one that I've heard other mothers of girls talk about—after all, as I've noted, the males of our species are hardwired to covet reproductive youth.

For all of us, our relationships with our mothers, mothers-in-law, siblings, daughters, husbands, boyfriends, and friends inform all the decisions we make about our look and style. My husband grew up in a family in which his mother never colored her hair, and both of his sisters have gray hair. His comfort with gray hair was slightly double-edged for me: on the one hand, the person to whom it actually matters whether I am "sexy" is accustomed to the women he loves having gray hair, but it's the women with whom he has a desexualized fraternal or filial love who have had the gray hair. And to compound the issue slightly, I am now considerably grayer than my husband—and really don't want to look like I'm older than he is. Which brings me back to the basic working assumption that gray hair automatically makes a person look a lot older—and less attractive.

Can Gray Be Sexy?

NOT LONG AFTER I'd announced to my husband that I planned to stop coloring, he came home and delivered what he intended as an upbeat insight into his own feelings about gray hair on women. He'd seen a thirty-five-ish woman on the subway with distinct gray-white streaks in her dark hair and said he found her "very hot" *because* of the gray. And that reminded him, he told me, of his assistant at a job a dozen years before, a woman who developed white streaks in her dark hair at age thirty. "And I actually found *that* extremely hot, too. Although she was sexy in general. Still is."

Great, honey! Thanks so much for sharing! Could you maybe have told me that before *I'd spent a zillion dollars coloring my hair?* But, in fact, it was interesting. And comforting. And kind of stopped me in my tracks. Maybe the truth is that men actually like gray hair (or at least don't mind it) and it is *women* who are their own worst enemies when it comes to liking and accepting gray as a suitable color. Without the image of a specific person in mind when asked in the abstract, "Do you find a woman with gray hair attractive?" it's easy to say no. A big part of this is the fact that, until we had the very sexy Helen Mirren as a role model during Oscar season this year, the typical mental image most men or women would have conjured of a woman with gray hair would have been their grandmothers. And sex and grandmothers just don't mix. Of course, if you ask if men with gray hair are sexy, George Clooney, Richard Gere, and Anderson Cooper come to mind.

I wondered if, were men presented with living, breathing, attractive female acquaintances who had gray hair, such as my husband's former assistant, rather than being asked in the abstract whether they like gray hair, they might have a different take. I decided to conduct a very informal poll of different-aged men I knew.

Scott, a slightly out of shape and slightly high-strung thirty-three-year-old manager of recording artists, was at the heartening end of the spectrum. "When I see gray hair on a woman younger than, say, her midfifties, it connotes wisdom in some odd way. Or a boldness to look a certain way that is attractive to me. And black hair with a touch of gray can also be really attractive."

A few weeks after talking with Scott, I bumped into John, a plain-white-button-down-oxford-shirt-chino-pant-wearing and highly flirtatious fifty-one-year-old television production executive, for the first time in almost a decade. The last time John had seen me, I'd had my ebony hair, so I was anxious about his response to my newly gray hair. He definitely noticed but didn't say anything about it. Which made me very self-conscious. When he asked me what I was up to and I'd nervously said, "I'm working on a book about going gray," he relieved me by professing real interest in the subject and suggesting we talk about it over lunch.

Given his general guy-on-the-make vibe, and also being still insecure in my newly gray hair, I was surprised to discover that John was into women with gray hair. "I've always loved a woman's gray hair, especially on a woman who's gone completely gray and dressed in a package where you wouldn't expect it. You know, we expect it from the last generation's 'grandmas,' like Aunt Bea on *The Andy Griffith Show*. But with a modern woman with a casual look, jeans and a T, a business suit, or an evening gown, it's great. For instance, you look great right now." *Phew*. Even with gray hair, I still rated his usual flirtation treatment. I was wearing a white cotton shirt, jeans, and an old black patent leather Agnès B. raincoat. "To me," he went on, "it's a real jolt to see a woman under forty, or in this day and age under fifty, who's confident enough to wear her hair gray or silver. It must be a drag when one is going gray and it's just a mess of all sorts of color. But once it's there, go for it. It's hot."

When I asked him if he thought other men shared his rather accepting point of view, he thought…not so much. "When I was younger, until maybe ten years ago, I figured that I had a pretty common, average outlook on almost everything regarding my views of women. So when I started hearing friends of mine say they wouldn't date a woman who didn't have a certain figure, a certain age, or a certain hair color, I realized I kind of stood alone. When I'm the only guy I can think of who married a second wife actually older than my first one, I guess I can figure that the gray-is-good crowd is smaller than I might think." I'm not sure if John is right in his belief, or whether it's just that there are so few younger women with gray hair that guys just don't think about it at all.

Dan, a single thirty-four-year-old journalist who has cut a wide swath through attractive young Manhattanites, claimed to be a hair-color agnostic. "I've never had a particular hair type I've preferred, and have dated curly-haired redheads to ironed-straight brunettes. I've also dated women who are starting to gray, which hasn't bothered me at all. With women who were beginning to gray who colored it, one or two times I've said that it didn't bother me at all—and they replied that it bothered *them*. Probably in the same way that I obsess considerably more about the presence of my back hair than anyone I've ever dated has." *Yes!* I think. Dan's got it right—it's women who obsess over their gray hair much more than men.

I wondered if maybe it was only the guys who worked in creative fields such as television or the music industry who were open-minded enough to find gray-haired women attractive. I met my old friend Henry, a fifty-one-year-old bachelor investment banker in Manhattan and serial dater of extremely attractive women (most of them a good ten or twenty years younger than he), for a drink. Henry had hardly any experience with gray-haired women, he said, not because he found them categorically unattractive, he insisted, but because single women in their forties had ex-husbands and children, and those were "complications" that tended to put him off. For a couple of months recently, he dated a woman only a few years younger than he, a divorcée with an older child, but she was (a) beautiful, (b) blond, and (c) a well-known movie actress.

Like Dan, Henry thinks that many, many women have ideas of what men find alluring that just aren't correct. "They dress for each other more than for men. They think we're responding to things we're not responding to." And even a brutally clear-eyed man like Henry insisted that men weren't as obsessed with sheer youth and prettiness as women assumed. "Remember," he said, "every time you see some beautiful woman walking down the street, some guy is tired of fucking her. If men are so superficial, how could a guy *ever* get tired of fucking a beautiful model? If it were *just* about beauty, that wouldn't happen. The way men read youth is about attitude and energy and vitality, the way a woman carries herself. Men respond to *that* kind of physicality." In other words...authenticity? "Well, I don't know any guy who really likes fake tits."

So far the men I'd talked with had lived in New York, so I called my good friend Jeff, a divorced, fifty-four-year-old, LA-based television writer, to see if men were as color-blind in LA. Jeff, of course, has *no* gray-haired colleagues and colors his own hair. He was definitively and defiantly un-PC. "Gray-haired women," he said, "run the risk of looking like they have given up. Only women who have been stunning all of their lives should consider running that risk. Some—very, very few—gray-haired women look great." Okay, fair enough. Thank God I don't live in LA.

But after talking at length to a half dozen men, I realized that, excepting show-business LA, hair color just isn't what guys ultimately care about. It's clear to me that we're stuck in a negative, mutually reinforcing trap: because women have completely internalized a false assumption that men respond to only a narrow range of beauty, women limit the range of possibility for men.

EMMYLOU HARRIS, the sixty-year-old country singer, is *the* great American icon for gray-haired female sexiness. Whenever I discussed with friends and acquaintances my decision to decolorize my hair and later to write this book, her name came up. As a thirty-six-year-old-professional-gardener friend said about her, "Take it from a young guy, gray hair is sexy—I think Emmylou Harris is about the sexiest thing out there."

She went gray very young and, in fact, dyed her hair for a while in her thirties. When I asked Emmylou if she thought certain kinds of men tended to be more attracted to women who let their hair appear in its natural gray or white, she talked to me about authenticity. She thinks *all* men find a "certain attractiveness to being natural....When it gets down to the nitty-gritty, when people start getting to know one another and you get into the realm of real human interaction, people want to be interested in the person whom it is comfortable to be with and who is passionate about life. We're all *enticed* by the physical — that's just biology. We're hardwired that way for the initial contact, but we all know that we are looking for someone to accept us and celebrate us for who we are. Who wants to put on an act twenty-four hours a day? What a nightmare it'd be to be afraid to have someone see us naked."

GRAY HAIR, she made me think, has become a form of public nakedness. Its very existence makes a statement to the world that the person wearing it tends to downplay artifice. When I go to parties now with my gray hair, I'm often the only woman in the room who isn't "wearing" any artificial color.

"I forget all about my gray hair," said my friend Susanna, "and then I'll catch a glimpse of myself in a street window, and I'll think, *This is a mistake.* I look my age. But I also have experiences that make me feel that I'm being too hard on myself. Recently I was walking down Walker Street [in the Tribeca neighborhood], and two young women decked out in hot pants, sandals with straps like vines wrapping up their legs, and *really* tight tops walked out of a building just as I was approaching. I stopped in my tracks to watch them. On the opposite side of the street, I noticed two male movers with their mouths equally agape, watching these women walk by. As I passed the men, one of them said to me, 'I like you better.' I must have looked shocked, because then he said, 'You're a real woman.'" And she has a hunch that her newish gray hair has, oddly, resulted in more social invitations, because hostesses now find her less sexually threatening. "I once had a friend who said that I was difficult to invite to a dinner party because other women didn't want me seated next to their husbands. Can you imagine?"

How we choose to present our hair color is complicated.

A wonderful seventy-five-year-old woman I met one afternoon at a mall on Long Island was passionate about why she still dyed her hair. Marjorie had huge, platinum cotton-candy hair and was dressed in tailored black pants, a chic black leather jacket, and a black-and-red scarf tied Dale Evans–style around her neck. She clearly devoted a great deal of attention to her packaging. I asked her if I could talk to her about her hair. "Oh, sure, honey, hair is the most important thing in my life as far as appearance — it doesn't stay the way I like it for very long, but I try." I asked if how she felt about her hair made her feel sexy. She thought for a minute. "If it makes you feel better about yourself, then you'll express more enthusiasm, and that can be sexy."

Toni, a colorist in a salon at the mall where I met Marjorie, thinks she knows without question why most of her clients dye their hair. "The women are either doing it for their husbands or else they're doing it to go to the clubs and cheat on their husbands. Either way it's for a man."

I DECIDED I WANTED MORE than just the stories and opinions of friends and strangers and celebrities. I wanted some hard data.

I'm borderline incompetent when it comes to statistics, so I enlisted the help of several others to design a survey that could probe people's attitudes about age and beauty and gray hair. First I called my friend Diana Rhoten, a dynamic forty-year-old social scientist with the National Science Foundation (with highlighted blond hair). Without question Diana is the single most can-do person I know. If I were ever to be stranded on a desert island, she'd be my first choice to be with after my family—I have no doubt that she'd figure out how to build our house, grow our crops, and jerry-rig some communications system that would get us off the island. Anyway, Diana turned me on to SurveyMonkey, a Web business that supports survey design and data gathering. Over a meatloaf dinner one night, she graciously taught me how to structure a survey.

Once the basics were done, I called on my sister-in-law, Kristi, a political scientist, and her brainiac grad-student daughter Emily to vet the questions I'd developed. Four hundred two women and ninety men around the country completed the rather exhaustive survey, which took respondents thirty minutes to fill out. All of my helpmates, who conduct polls on a regular basis, were surprised by the robustness of the response rate. It was no real surprise to me—people care passionately about the way they look.

In particular I wanted to answer the $64,000 question: exactly how much older does gray hair make people look, and is it regarded as inherently unattractive?

I also enlisted (okay, coerced) six friends—two thirtysomethings, two fortysomethings, and two fiftysomethings, two of whom have naturally brown hair, one who's gray, three who use artificial color—to pose for pictures. I posed, too. Then I had the images digitally manipulated, using Photoshop software, to produce fourteen images: all seven of us with brown hair *and* all seven of us with gray.

Each survey contained a randomly selected version of each of us. In other words, a given survey respondent saw each of our faces only once, either as a brown-haired person *or* as a gray-haired one. As a sort of "control," and to test the conventional wisdom that gray hair on men isn't nearly as problematic, one of the fifty-year-olds was male.*

WE ASKED OUR RESPONDENTS about each of the seven people pictured on their surveys: *Would you fix this person up with a friend? How old do you think this person is?*

My assumption going in was that people with gray hair would be deemed less attractive—that is, less likely to be chosen as a fix-up for a friend. And in a section of the survey where I simply asked women if they thought men found women with gray hair less attractive, the respondents, by a two-to-one margin, said yes. But the results of the almost-identical-twin photo test went the other way, completely surprising me. For Barbara, who has a lot of dark hair, the photoshopped very gray hair did indeed make her perceived as less fix-uppable, and for the fake-gray thirty-eight-year-old Emily T., there was a tiny disadvantage. But for the rest of us, four out of the six women, there was a modest but consistent *advantage* in fix-up-ability for the gray-haired versions.

*To see the photographs, please go to www.AnneKreamer.com/book_photos_test .html.

However, the more fundamental conventional wisdom was borne out: a color other than gray or white does make people look younger by about three years on average. For Tom and Allison, the effect was just two years; for Bonnie and me, it was closer to three; and for Emily O., it was nearly four. People guessed that Emily T. was, on average, five years younger with her natural brown hair. And Barbara was reckoned to be seven and a half years younger with brown hair versus gray.

When I told Barbara the results of the survey, she replied, "I have always thought, *Just let me look five years younger.* So there you go. I'm not changing my routine."

The good news for Barbara was that people thought she looked years younger than she actually was, regardless of hair color—exactly the opposite of Allison, who, with gray hair, was estimated to be six or nine years older than her true age, which was thirty-one at the time. Indeed, gray hair made only the youngest of the women and the one man—Allison, Emily T., and Tom—appear older than they *actually* were. With my hair photoshopped brown, my average estimated age was forty-five, and with my gray hair, the average was just shy of forty-eight. I was nearly fifty when the picture was taken.

And to me the data clearly indicate that when gray hair is age-appropriate (from our forties onward), *we don't actually fool people* about our age when we dye it. When women in their thirties have gray hair, it seems, people assume they are older because it's unusual to have gray hair at that age.

So my gray hair doesn't make me look older than I am; it just allows people to guess my true age a little more accurately. I know that's definitely a glass-half-full way of looking at it. But I'm willing to pay the price and make the trade-off—I'll give up that three-year illusion in exchange for the luxury of being a bit more straightforward with myself and the world about who I am and how old I really am.

Interestingly, even though artificial color has become almost universal, people are still reluctant to say they dye their hair in order to fool people—that is, to appear more youthful. Of the respondents to my survey who color their hair, fewer than one in four, when asked why they do so, said it was to look younger and (therefore) sexier—whereas 50 percent said the reason was "just aesthetics," as though preferring brown or red or blond is simply a matter of taste, nothing to do with faux youth. And when those people were asked why they started coloring in the first place, only one in six came straight out and admitted their motive was to look younger. Even if people proudly and openly declare that they color their hair, they remain ambivalent about their true motives. And it seems that, in spite of all the antiaging cultural indoctrination, most of us feel a little guilty admitting that something as superficial as wanting to look younger motivates our behavior.

"Dating" — My Three-City Match.com Road Test

As I was in the middle of my survey research, I realized that there was another, closer-to-the-bone experiment I could conduct to test whether having gray hair was a detriment to dating for a woman my age. I could offer up myself on an Internet dating site — or, rather, fudge my marital and parental status (it's the Internet, isn't it?) and pretend to be available for dates. And even better, with the miracle of Photoshop, I could do it as both a gray-haired fifty-year-old and a brunette fifty-year-old.

I'd post the same photographs of myself I'd used in the online survey. The accompanying profile, except for the divorced-and-no-children part, would be accurate. My plan was to post first with gray hair and leave it up for three weeks, then take it down for a few months. Then I'd post the same description and the same photo, this time with brown hair. I figured that if I was honest about my age and the *only* substantive variable that changed from one profile to the next was the color of my hair, then I could test pretty definitively if gray hair alone was a determining factor in attractiveness to men.

I chose Match.com for my experiment because its membership of fifteen million is more interested in no-strings-attached dating than are members of sites such as eHarmony, where users are explicitly hoping to find a mate. I was trying to create as pure a test as possible of gray versus brunette as a basis for datability, and I didn't want to mislead anyone into thinking I wanted to get married.

Even though I knew it was a good idea for the purposes of this book, I was unnerved by the prospect of actually doing it. I had no real idea how Internet "communities" worked, let alone the protocols of online dating. I became really anxious about telling my family, particularly my husband, that I was going to put my face and personal details out on the Web to try to (virtually) meet strange men. Kurt is not an overly jealous person, but I imagined that this would test even his limits.

There was no easy way to handle the discussion, so with genuine trepidation, I announced to the entire family over dinner one night what I planned to do — I wanted the kids there so they could be on "my side" on the off chance that Kurt really hated the idea. Thank God my husband is a writer with a sense of mischief, and a sort of data nerd besides, because he instantly got the idea of trying to quantify the level of interest my gray-haired image would generate versus my brown-haired one. He was a little unsettled by the idea of me pretending to date ("In the movie version of this," he said, "you actually meet a guy and fall in love with him"), but he understood my need to do the experiment and ultimately endorsed it. My teenage girls just thought it was one more weird, embarrassing thing their weird, embarrassing mother was doing.

The day I finally sat down to join Match.com and write my profile, my heart started to race. It was scary. I was going to thrust myself into a public forum, asking thousands of men to judge and rate me—and what was even more terrifying was that friends or acquaintances might actually see my picture and think that my husband and I had split up. ("That's the first act of the movie version," Kurt said.)

As it happened, that same week I came across a release on the Hispanic PR Wire that led me to believe my gray hair could be a deterrent in the imaginary dating I was about to undertake.

When it comes to making a good first impression in the dating scene, online matchmaking can prove to be the most difficult. Just in time for the New Year, Just for Men Haircolor is releasing findings from a national "First Impressions" Survey to help singles find their perfect cyber sweetie. The blind online survey of seven thousand online daters... found that the biggest turnoff for a cyber dater is gray hair. An overwhelming 86 percent of women and 91 percent of men said they would not date someone with gray hair, preferring instead someone who looks younger.

Oh, dear.

I had given zero thought to how I might answer all the Match. com profile questions. In fact, I'd had no idea that there *were* profile questions. I decided that I wanted all of my answers to generate the largest possible response pool, so I agonized for a day or two about my screen name, finally deciding to use elements from the parlor game in which you use the name of your first pet and first street address to find your "porn-star name" — "Snowball Veranda" or "Muffin St. James." The first street I lived on was Pennsylvania, and the house number was 6450. My screen name, Pennsylvania6450, was born. I hoped it was neutral in a good way, Pennsylvania having no distinctly regional connotations, and 6450 an apparently random number.

I was nervous, maybe foolishly, about giving out my real birthday online, so I used my month and year but picked a random alternate day. What really mattered was to be clear that I was fifty. At first I said I was separated because it just felt too upsetting to put in writing that I was divorced. (Have I mentioned that I'm superstitious?) But my husband convinced me that no guy would want to get embroiled with someone who was separated—too messy, too complicated, too "not ready"—so divorced I'd have to be. I also hated erasing my children from the picture, but the same argument held—kids implied complications, and I wanted the universe of potential men to think I was minimally complicated and available at the drop of a hat.

I began to wonder how truthful anybody's profile was. Once again, the spectrum stretching from honesty to dishonesty, along which we all live, had surfaced. I was feeling very uncertain: a will to candor made me quit coloring my hair, yet I was lying online to try to discover the truth about gray hair. I hoped the ends justified the means.

For the rest of the profile questions, I was truthful but also didn't want to look like I was trying too hard. I wanted to include things that made me seem a youthful and fun fifty-year-old. When I was done, I couldn't imagine anyone wanting to date me — if I were reading my profile, I'd think I was some kind of emotionally inaccessible android. And I just had to pray that no one I knew would happen to come across me. It was *really* disturbing to hit the "send" button.

This is what I posted in my profile:

What do you do for fun?
I watch Jon Stewart, *Deadwood,* and *The O.C.* I read mysteries, am getting marginally better at crosswords.

Favorite local hot spots or travel destinations?
I like to go lots of places and prefer quirky to glitzy. A great day would be walking through an unfamiliar neighborhood anywhere, discovering some shop with

one-of-a-kind things: books, objects, old clothes — and lucking into a cozy restaurant.

Favorite things?

Meatloaf, aquamarine blue, no rain (I like sunny weather), big dogs, black cats, Death Cab for Cutie, Philip Glass, jeans, yoga.

Describe yourself and your perfect match to our community.

It's easiest for me to describe myself in terms of different media: I'm both Stephen Colbert and Jim Lehrer, Capote and King Kong, more Whole Foods than Burger King, and don't believe things are black or white. My match is someone similar.

In all of the more generic, "check one" multiple-choice answers, I tried to be honest but also to open myself up to the largest number of respondents — to emphasize my more populist, regular-girl aspects. I checked that I liked sports, even though I'd literally rather go to the dentist than watch sports on TV — I do like *playing* sports. I said I didn't care about men's levels of education, income, religion, or any of the rest of it — again, my intention being to maximize the pool for potential dates for the purposes of the experiment. And I didn't answer any of the mortifying, *Playboy* Playmate–ish questions about what turned me on — long hair, piercings, thunderstorms...sorry, no answer.

And for the purposes of the experiment, I had my Photoshop helper slightly whiten my hair in the photo so that it would be even more unambiguous in the small image on the computer that I had gray hair.

That first night, my husband and daughter Lucy and I went online together to see what the men and women of Match.com looked like and what they said about themselves. We all hovered around the computer and speculated. Did we think they could smell me as a fake?

Out of the several hundred fortyish-to-late-fiftyish women we browsed, only two had gray or white hair, while about a quarter of the men seemed to have gray or graying hair. My smug, I-don't-need-to-check-out-the-online-dating-universe-because-I'm-married assumption had been that the people we'd see online would look creepy, "loserish." I now feel really stupid to have had such an uninformed idea. What surprised all of us, including our FaceBook-MySpace-fluent daughter, was how regular and inviting most of the people looked. Indeed, scanning the prospective dating universe of women living within a two-mile radius of our house, my husband found lots of women he'd "date." How gratifying. "I wonder," he said, "if any of these are mothers from the kids' school. And do you think some of them know people we know?" Which caused my anxiety about a friend seeing me on Match.com to spike.

During the first three days of my gray profile being posted, about a hundred men looked at me—and I got three "winks." "Wink" is Match.com's leering term of art for when someone is interested enough to exchange e-mails with you. They "wink" you. Or you "wink" them. Not only did I *hate* the word but, unlike the relatively attractive men I'd seen the first night, I also thought the first few guys who "winked" me were frankly sort of skevey-looking. The first was a fifty-six-year-old who looked like a guy you'd see sitting alone at a bar in the early afternoon.

Now that I was winked, I realized I had to have an MO about how to respond. What to *say* to the grizzled fifty-six-year-old who may be e-mailing me from his local public library? I felt bad that I was leading men on even slightly and didn't want to extend the charade for each one any longer than necessary. After all, I was interested in them only as data, not as individual would-be fake dates. Thank goodness Match.com provided a simple, generic "Not Interested" reply option. I overstepped my boundary only once, when a hunky-looking thirty-two-year-old guy whose profile said he was interested in meeting women eighteen to thirty-four winked me. I e-mailed him back, asking why he winked someone who was fifty if he was interested in women younger than thirty-five. I must have sounded like a cop (or some twisted version of the sexual-predators sting operations on *Dateline NBC*) trying to entrap him. Clearly I didn't have the language of dating on my mind. I never heard from him again.

I received a total of three hundred "looks" and seven "winks" from men of all ages during the three weeks that my gray-haired photo was posted. Two of my seven winks were from African Americans. I wasn't sure what to make of that, but perhaps my nonstandard hair color as an "issue" was overshadowed and mooted by the skin-color issue. I have no idea what kind of a response I might have gotten had I actually winked anyone myself. I didn't feel it would be right for me to initiate an encounter and misrepresent myself to that degree. But the number of responses was surprising—and, frankly, flattering.

I also found the online community interesting. The incomes of people who winked me ranged from $25,000 to about $100,000; the professions, from sales executive to gardener. I approved of the whole process more than I expected to—it felt accessible and open, and even if lots of people were fibbing (as I was), it still encouraged a kind of democratic bumping together that could only be good. I'm lucky to live in a city where it is relatively easy to meet people at classes and lectures and clubs, but if I lived in a more isolating rural or suburban place and wanted to meet men, I would definitely do online dating.

After a three-month hiatus, I posted my brown-haired picture and the identical profile—divorced New Yorker, no kids—on Match.com. To try to throw off anyone who'd looked at gray-haired me and might come across the new image, I decided to change my screen name to Kansas1246. I thought that if anyone actually busted me on my new hair color, I'd tell them that because I hadn't had much luck as a gray-haired person, I had decided to color my hair to improve my chances. No one did.

The results this time were a shock. Over the course of the first week, I got fourteen looks and only two winks. And during the entire three-week period, the brown-haired me got *no* additional winks and only seventy looks total.

In other words, I had received more than four times the initial interest with my silver hair, and more than three times as many winks. I suspected my experiment must be somehow flawed. The idea that men were significantly more attracted to the gray-haired me just didn't make sense. Had I exhausted the universe of New York–area men on Match.com? I decided to replicate the experiment in different geographic areas, also switching the order in which I posted the different-colored photos. So I "moved" to Chicago and this time started with my brown-haired image. After three weeks, the brown-haired me had forty-nine looks and five winks from Chicagoans. And then, with my gray hair, I got seventy-nine looks and five winks during the subsequent three-week test period — including my first wink ever from someone who actually proposed to meet for a drink, a good-looking guy in his midforties.

For the final and, I assumed, most challenging test, I posted my gray-haired image as a resident of Los Angeles. Over the three weeks, I got forty-seven looks and four winks — one from a thirty-three-year-old African American, two from Latinos in their forties (take *that,* Hispanic PR Wire), and the other from a twenty-nine-year-old Greek American. As opposed to the uniformly white, middle-aged guys who winked me in Chicago, all of the LA guys were objectively *GQ*-hot and all but one significantly younger than I. In any event, during my three weeks as a brown-haired potential online date in LA, I had the same staggeringly counterintuitive result as in New York and

Chicago—only twenty-three looks, all from men in their fifties, and not a single wink.

Overall, I got three times as many Match.com "looks" with my gray hair, which might be attributable in part simply to the freak factor—because it's rare to see a gray-haired woman on the site, some men may have clicked simply out of curiosity. But in each of the three cities, I also got as many or more "winks" with gray hair as with brown—and nationally, twice as many "winks."

Crazy. Whatever the reasons, to men across America, I am apparently lots more attractive as a gray-haired fifty-year-old than as a brown-haired fifty-year-old. I was flabbergasted—and very, very pleased, not just for the sake of my own vanity but also as one small but powerful refutation of the conventional wisdom. I really felt like I was onto something. In the abstract, as I found in my online survey, people reflexively think that gray hair connotes aging and is less attractive, but when faced with the specific reality of it, we find that *it just isn't true.* With this scientifically confirmed knowledge, I began to walk down the street with a new level of confidence about my decision to go gray.

But *why?* I couldn't imagine this result was somehow unique to the way I happened to look. Maybe the "authenticity" was appealing, the implicit truthfulness and I-am-who-I-am self-confidence. Or maybe some men were betting that a gray-haired woman on Match.com was so desperate to hook up that their odds of scoring would be high.

The last of these possibilities inevitably raised a prurient question: is there a subset of men (or women) for whom gray hair is not just a neutral factor in sexual fantasy but rather a specific turn-on? I Googled "gray-haired women porn sites," and 194,000 hits popped up, with names such as "Old Swinger Pussy" and "Old Mature Sluts" (and, oddly, "Gray Hair: Job Asset or Liability?" from CBS News). I browsed deeper and discovered that the answer to my question was ambiguous—there definitely is a thriving market for "mature" pornography. The women pictured looked older than forty, but in my (limited) tour of this subculture, I found only one site that showed women with gray hair, and they were all over sixty. The women in the mature sites were overwhelmingly blond, and even the oldest had shaved their pubic regions—a topic for a different book on curious twenty-first-century hair-grooming trends.

A Night on the Town

THE CYBERSPACE pseudodating experience actually gave me enough confidence to decide to see what it felt like to try and meet men in person. I would go barhopping. "Okay," my husband said when I broached this upping of the ante, "and *now* the movie turns from romantic comedy into a darker, edgier thriller." He dropped his voice to imitate a movie-trailer narrator's gravelly voice-over: "Where playful fibs and fantasy turn into the unbelievably awful truth." But he didn't veto the idea.

I fancied that I might replicate in real life the gray-hair/brown-hair experiment I'd explored online. I went out to buy a brown wig, in the same cut and color as I'd styled my hair before going gray, and planned to go to some bars with the fake brown hair and to others with my natural gray.

To buy the wig, I went to a tiny hole-in-the-wall store on 14th Street in Manhattan that caters principally to African

American women and young hipsters of all ethnicities—needless to say, I didn't fit the profile of their usual customers. A staid-looking, middle-aged white woman walking through the door was cause for a degree of hilarity on the part of the staff. Which made me happy. I have loved, while researching this book, being forced to move outside my usual comfort zones—approaching strangers and phoning people I don't know to talk with them about their lives and hair, exposing myself to ridicule and some modest excitement on Match.com, going into places entirely off my beaten path.

I think one of the things that terrifies me the most about getting older is a fear that I'll just settle into some dull and, forgive me, gray routine in life. Get up, make breakfast, read the papers, do the household chores, do my work, make dinner, do the dishes, take out the trash, watch a little TV, go to bed. Repeat. And repeat. And repeat. That my choice to embrace my "grayness" has given me a pretext for interacting with a larger world is personally huge. I've had real fun; engaged with family, friends, and strangers in wholly new, intimate, and personal ways; and been forced to scrutinize my own fears and insecurities...being old, irrelevant, or "out of it," or just looking tapped out and ugly. I've actually begun to internalize and understand for real that it isn't so much how we think others think we look that is important; it's how we *feel.* I know, I know, every women's magazine, talk show, and self-help book says the exact same thing, but I needed to experience it firsthand to believe it.

Walking into the wig shop didn't make me feel like Jennifer

Garner in *Alias,* but some of my buttoned-down, blend-in-with-the-crowd default behaviors were loosening up.

A tall black woman with closely cropped, dyed-platinum hair was completing her purchase of a long, curly dark-brown wig as I approached the counter. Her instant change, from looking like the rapper Eve one minute to Beyoncé the next, was amazing—and she looked fabulous. The two young male salesclerks were having fun with her, and I got into the spirit of my mission. I told the guys my plan to go to bars and compare what happened in two different looks—and they *loved* the idea. They also gave me a tutorial on how to put my wig on, since I hadn't a clue how to make it look at all natural.

I knew I couldn't go out barhopping by myself—it'd been years since I'd done it, and I also knew that even suggesting that I go out alone would be asking way too much of my easygoing husband. But it occurred to me that going with him would be deeply awkward for both of us—I certainly couldn't even begin to try to flirt effectively with him lurking in the background.

I enlisted one of our closest friends, Billy, a foreign correspondent who is experienced at dealing with unfamiliar places and deft at getting people to talk to him, and who is also a good drinking buddy from back in the days when I used to do some pretty good drinking. And beyond the expediency of having a friend to "chaperone" the test, I realized that having a male eyewitness to help digest the experiences of the night would be helpful. I thought another female point of view would be essential, so I asked my friend Rachel, an ebullient woman about my age, if she'd be up for a night out on the town. She was game. At the minimum I thought that the three of us going out would be fun and that with their help I might have better luck meeting men.

I wanted to go high to low, restaurants and fancy hotels to regular bars. Billy suggested that we go out on one of the nights of March Madness, the NCAA basketball play-offs — his thinking was that the games would ensure the hetero guys would be out in droves. I hadn't been to a bar in an up-for-action mode since the Carter administration, so I had zero idea of where to go or how to dress. I relied on Billy to chart our course.

One night the week before the outing, while waiting for a dinner table, I started feeling like an anthropologist observing the young and not-so-young people crowded around the restaurant's bar. The restaurant, in the trendy lower Manhattan Meatpacking District, had just opened and was the red-hot gustatory center for that month. The people at the bar were very definitely there *to be seen.* And the scene was the opposite of the *Star Wars* we're-all-freaky-aliens cantina. The women uniformly were wearing tight, super-low-cut, slightly flared jeans; low-cut tight shirts; and pointy, kitten-heeled shoes. (My sixteen-year-old had taught me the term "kitten-heeled.") Every single one of them had a very shiny little bag with lots of metal studs and chains. They all seemed to have Jennifer Aniston circa 2003 hair. Their tight asses and abs jostled as they swiveled to see who might be elbowing up next to them.

I inventoried my own clothing options and body type and calculated how I'd fit in at that bar. I owned the approximately correct items, but my stuff looked like '80s artifacts, and not in a hip retro way. My jeans were classic Gap cut, my shirts and shoes, J.Crew. I'd be lumpen next to these sleek women. Not a chance in the world that a guy in that situation would give me a glance, let alone a second look. I found my enthusiasm for the escapade—that is, the field study—waning.

Rachel and I had a whole series of e-mails about what to wear. She decided on a simple black dress and black pumps, but I didn't want to look very different from how I'd go out with my husband or friends, and I certainly didn't want to look like I was trying too hard to pick up guys—the whole point of the exercise was to see what might happen without too much effort. So I opted for jeans, not the two-hundred-dollar 7 for All Mankind jeans worn by the women at the restaurant bar but a tried-and-true pair of Levi's; a crisp white shirt—since I'm a woman who wears turtlenecks in every month but August, my one concession to overt "sexiness" was to open one more button of my shirt than felt comfortable—a three-quarter-length flowered jacket; and green boots.

And the brown wig? No matter how hard I tried, it just looked ridiculously fake. As Rachel and I studied the bewigged me in my bathroom mirror, she said, "You look like a Hasid's wife." Which wasn't really the image I was going for. I ditched the wig, put on mascara, and was set. Without mentioning it to my husband, I also decided to leave my wedding rings at home—entirely in the interest of research. (When I admitted to him afterward that I'd gone wedding ring–less, he replied, deadpan,

"That's okay—I had a couple of hookers come over while you were out.")

This particular Friday was an early spring–like night after a very long winter, and the streets were practically Mardi Gras festive, with people out for fun. On our walk to my car, a group of twentysomething guys cruised by, and one of the boys leaned out the window and shouted, "Hey, ladies, how *you* doin' tonight?" It was a good omen.

We picked up Billy, a fifty-three-year-old, 6'2", slightly professorial manly man—and off we went to the Maritime Hotel bar in Manhattan. The three of us approached the bar together to calm my jittery nerves, to let Rachel and Billy get to know each other, and to fine-tune the strategy. I'd given a lot of thought over the week to how I could best ensure that I'd get some interaction with men. One of my thoughts was that Billy could go in first and hang out with a few of the guys at the bar while Rachel and I could arrive a bit later and sit at the opposite end. He could then get the guys he was with to discuss whether they thought "those ladies" were "doable." Or, I thought, he could just watch and take notes from a guy's point of view while Rachel and I tried to see if any men would attempt to pick us up. But of course we totally improvised.

It was a typical young professional scene at the Maritime, people under forty, all still in their work clothes, letting loose on the first warm Friday night of the year. The Maritime, named because it was once the national headquarters for the Maritime Union, is a groovy place in groovy Chelsea. The building is funky, a white ceramic tower dotted with porthole-style windows, and feels like a retro ocean liner. Most of the people were outdoors in a courtyard filled with blue-and-white-striped umbrella-topped tables, but it seemed like only couples or large groups of friends were there. Hoping to have better luck finding single guys, we headed indoors to the restaurant and bar.

There were a few pods of men around the bar, so that was where we gravitated, but frankly I couldn't tell if they were straight. How awkward would it be if I spent the night trying to pick up a gay guy? Oh, God—I was *so* out of my depth. My little "experiment" was going to be a whole lot more challenging than I had blithely fantasized. I'd forgotten just how hard it was to strike up a conversation with people I didn't know. And I had thirty years of "don't mess with me, I'm married" New Yorker vibes to undo in a single night.

When Michael, the Toby Maguire–esque bartender, came to take our order, I worked up my courage and asked him what he thought of women with gray hair. "My mother never dyed her hair in her life," he said. "My parents were old hippies, Berkeley '67, '68, and I don't like girls with too much makeup. I just don't have the taste for that type. People with gray hair are *into* it, I think." *Especially those of us writing books on the subject,* I didn't interject. "Frankly," he went on, "all of us make snap judgments, and it seems to me that everyone is always wearing a costume anyway. So, to me, gray hair is a statement that the costume is actually the lack of a costume." Michael was saying gray hair sends a message that what you see is what you get.

I swallowed my dignity and asked him for tips on how I might get, uh, picked up. He gave me clear guidelines. Don't go to clubs—everyone there is using a fake ID and is about eighteen. And go by yourself. If you are with friends, you won't look approachable. *Right! Check! Can do.* I would have to peel off from Rachel and Billy if I hoped to produce any results. I still wanted their point of view, so I asked them if they'd mind sitting separately from me at our next stop.

After ducking in and out of several bars and restaurants where the majority of people were couples, we ended up at Pete's Tavern, a famous old New York bar near Gramercy Park. Pete's was perfect—narrow and dark-paneled, with dining in the back room, a long bar, several overhead TVs showing basketball, and a jukebox playing Neil Young, Van Morrison, The Doors. *Music! Right!* Another important mood-setter for meeting guys. I snagged the one open seat near the front door while my friends, following the Maritime bartender's instructions, went to the back of the room.

I sat down next to a guy in his thirties who was watching the game. And then froze—now what? It was clear to me that the guy wanted to talk but didn't know how to break the ice. So, genius that I am, I asked, "What's the score?" I sensed his relief that I had made the first overture and felt encouraged to ask him what he did for a living. Central casting couldn't have sent me a better man—think Tom Cruise in *Top Gun*. My Tom was a thirty-nine-year-old electronics specialist in the merchant marine (sort of sexy), with top secret clearance (very sexy, although per-haps untrue). Plus, he was in town visiting his sick father (aw). He was intelligent, youngish, old-fashioned but high-tech, and good-looking—plus he was devoted to his father. *Jackpot!*

We talked and flirted for about fifteen minutes. When I asked what he thought about my gray hair, he said, "Men just don't care about that."

And then, finally, I came clean about what I was doing—because it had become clear to me that if I'd really wanted to go home with him that night, he'd be up for it. I already felt creepy enough having misrepresented myself this far and didn't want to lead him on any further. Fortunately, because he did seem like a decent guy, he took the news well—and then seemed interested in what it was like to write a book. It was altogether a charming interaction and one that made me feel good about life.

So after only two hours, I'd had two very cute, very nice young guys tell me that gray hair didn't matter to them, one of whom had been pretty clearly prepared to prove his indifference. In fact, I began to think gray hair might actually be an advantage in a dating situation, a means of dispensing with one layer of dissem-bling and artificiality and bet-hedging that frightens people off—a signal that says *I'm not lying* and *I'm confident* from the get-go.

As a final stop after dropping Billy back home, Rachel and I visited a lesbian bar called Cattyshack in Park Slope, Brooklyn, which is described by *New York* magazine as follows: "The weekend parties, which feature thong-clad girls writhing on stripper poles, are hip enough to pull in a mix of *faux*-hawks, bridge-and-tunnel singles, celesbians, and even a spattering of boys." I didn't know what a "hawk" was, let alone a "*faux*-hawk," but I was curious to see if my gray hair would be unusual in the lesbian bar and if I'd get approached there. Short gray hair is, after all, something of a stereotypical lesbian look.

We paid our cover charge and strolled in. Although I'd read about the pole dancers, I was still astounded and slightly embarrassed to see a pretty young topless woman up on the bar, bumping and grinding and writhing, working the room. Rachel and I were a good ten years older than anyone else in the place, and even in my jeans I felt overdressed. I don't think anyone even looked at us — it's like we had a We're Not Actually Gay force field around us. And *no one else* in the joint had gray hair, by the way.

The next day I asked Billy for his take on our night on the town. We had a long, funny e-mail exchange about the particulars — but then he delivered his bottom line. "Here's the thing I think the evening confirmed — think European, or, if you like, Parisian. Doesn't matter how old you are, if you've got wit and presence about it — flirting is *fun*. People do it because they like it. And they like you back if you're good at it. Maybe *especially* if you've got gray hair — it proves you've had a life, and you're not 'going gentle,' as Dylan Thomas would put it."

Is Gray Hair Illegal in Hollywood?

There is no professional milieu in which the currency of physical attractiveness is more important than in show business, where an appearance of youthfulness and one's livelihood are explicitly, inextricably linked. Several serious actresses have become known for evidently eschewing plastic surgery as they age—Meryl Streep (fifty-nine), Sigourney Weaver (fifty-eight), Susan Sarandon (sixty-one)—but apart from Jamie Lee Curtis (forty-nine), who is on a kind of one-woman campaign for middle-aged authenticity, there are no famous American actresses with naturally gray hair. *None.* Which is amazing.

The screenwriter Bruce Feirstein, who lives in LA (and has three James Bond movies to his credit), gave me his take. "Hollywood—movies, TV, mass entertainment—has always been focused on youth and vanity. And from the very beginning, actors—and particularly actresses—have always had a short shelf life. There's always somebody new and younger and fresher coming up.

"When I was younger, I had a great moment of revelation about this with regard to an actress friend of mine. When we were in our late twenties and early thirties, she was a giant star. And then, in her midthirties, those sexy-leading-lady roles began to dry up. At the time, her friends fretted that this was due to her sometimes demanding personality. We would talk about what we had to do to 'help her.' But then one day I realized—it wasn't her fault. It was just inevitable that someone would come along, ten years younger, and fit the same basic archetype."

And, of course, the double standard concerning age for men and women in the movies is staggering. Gray-haired actors such as Richard Gere, George Clooney, Harrison Ford, Clint Eastwood, and Paul Newman have all continued to get sexy-leading-man roles into their late forties, fifties, and sixties. For women meant to be convincingly sexy on-screen, fifty is pretty much the sell-by date. What has rather suddenly happened, for instance, to the careers of Michelle Pfeiffer and Jessica Lange and Meg Ryan? They all made the mistake of turning forty-five.

But none of them is heavy, or very saggy—or gray. "It isn't so much a spoken pressure," a movie-industry executive told me, "but one that's as much a part of LA as sunshine: *You can't let yourself go.*" And by "go," he means "appear to age at normal speed."

I immediately thought of my old friend Jeff, the Ivy League–educated TV writer in Santa Monica who'd told me bluntly that gray hair signaled to him that a woman had "given up."

"You're an actress, or an actor," the executive said, "and you're going to be forty feet tall on the screen. Talent is more or less a given, and somewhat unquantifiable—if there are six actresses who are more or less qualified for the role, it's always going to go to the one that the director or studio thinks is most attractive. To ignore this is to be naive. Ditto to railing against it. Directors will often tell people to lose ten pounds or go to a trainer and tone that body. But is that really any different than a book editor in New York City telling a brilliant writer to cut two chapters from a novel? In both cases, the editor and the director are just trying to make the final product better. And in both cases, the talent is a given."

The unfortunate difference for actors and actresses, of course, is that they are obliged to *be* that convincingly young, sexy product 24-7, even when they're not acting, in order to convince the industry and the wider world that they can *play* young and sexy. And the unfortunate difference for the rest of us is that, with actresses, as opposed to novelists or any other cultural figures, we internalize the perfectionist standards imposed on them as our own—and try to live up to a standard for which we lack not only the genes but the vast Hollywood tool kit.

When they're performing, actresses, unlike actors, are often wearing wigs, which makes maintaining continuity from scene five to scene twenty-seven easier, and makes the prep both faster and easier on the actresses' real hair. And so when women in the audience, mostly unaware of this particular fakery, find themselves wishing for hair that looks more like Nicole Kidman's in *The Interpreter,* or Meg Ryan's in *You've Got Mail,* they're yearning for a literally unattainable artificial ideal.

And what would happen if, when they *weren't* working, gray-haired actresses appeared in public — on talk shows, on red carpets, at stores and restaurants — as gray-haired women? Would they be offered fewer or less interesting or less remunerative parts? Maybe, maybe not, but apparently none of them is willing to risk it. We are all caught up in wanting to perpetuate the fantasy that none of us is aging. And the more that America's tens of millions of naturally gray- and white-haired women color their hair, the more pressure there will be on our celebrated icons of beauty to deny the reality as well and *live* the fantasy — and then, on TV and in the movies and magazines, that fantasy will be in turn reinforced for the anonymous tens of millions. It's an infinite feedback loop.

Given that a relatively modest studio movie now costs $100 million to make and market, and putting on any new network series is a multimillion-dollar bet, risk-averse studios and networks are obviously hesitant to test this chicken-and-egg conventional wisdom too aggressively. But I wonder if the boomer audience in particular might not turn out in droves if good Hollywood movies and series were routinely produced starring older, sexy, powerful women. One would think that the recent success of Diane Keaton in *Something's Gotta Give* ($267 million worldwide box office) and *The Family Stone* ($92 million), or Meryl Streep in *The Devil Wears Prada* ($257 million), or Helen Mirren in *The Queen* ($261 million) would drive that point home to executives.

Anna Quindlen experienced firsthand how hard it is to get movies made with meaty roles for older women. In her recent bestselling novel *Blessings,* the central character is an old woman looking back on her well-lived life, and Quindlen particularly loved her. "I couldn't believe I hadn't done that before," she said, meaning create an older protagonist. "I had every stage of life in this character, and people really responded powerfully and viscerally to her. But in Hollywood no one even *thought* about doing a feature about a woman of that age." *Blessings* was ultimately made into a TV movie starring Mary Tyler Moore for CBS, the network recently known for its older audience—and nearly every review mentioned how the curly gray wig that Moore wore in the role completely transformed her. "You could talk about *Driving Miss Daisy* until the cows came home," said Quindlen, "but no one in Hollywood was going to touch *Blessings* [as a feature film]." In her next novel, *Rise and Shine,* the main characters are forty-seven and forty-three, and Quindlen has been fortunate enough to have the producer Lydia Pilcher (who has produced all of Mira Nair's films) option the theatrical rights for the book. Quindlen thinks the sale was helped by the fact that the producer is a woman and the directors being considered for the film are also women.

The actress Frances McDormand told me she feels fortunate

that her professional life has never been based "on being a babe. I was barely an ingenue. I'm not classically feminine.

"I wore prosthetic breasts in *Raising Arizona* [1987] because my character lived in a trailer park and had five kids, and she needed to have the blousiness and bounciness of large breasts. But of course then I started getting scripts for women with large breasts. And I actually started taking my prosthetic breasts to auditions in a box—I wanted to prove that I could *act* like a woman with large breasts. Until I got to one audition where one of the casting directors asked, 'Have you ever considered having your breasts done? Because we could budget that.' I mean, to think that I would cut my breasts open to get *one job.*

"Through my early years as an actress, I was told that I was too funny-looking, and too flat-chested, so I made myself indispensable in those areas of the profession based on being interesting. And this has allowed me to mature professionally and work continuously because I didn't have to remain locked into one persona. If I'd started out my career as the ingenue or leading lady, I would *have* to have been vain, but a character actor has much more latitude." Since the wider world was ready to "discover" her in her thirties and forties, she said, that latitude has powered her career. "When an actress puts on weight or puts black on her teeth or puts on a pregnancy pillow and plays a cop in a brown suit, it becomes a big deal—those are images that people aren't used to seeing."

McDormand has thought a lot about her non-movie-star

looks and being a middle-aged actor. "When I started being cast as the love interest, it was often for the benefit of the male characters like Robert De Niro in *City by the Sea* [2002] or Michael Douglas in *Wonder Boys* [2000]" — by which she means she gave them depth and gravitas because she *isn't* a babe. "It's different being cast opposite me than it is being cast opposite Sharon Stone. I've been in roles that deal with sexuality, but the only time I really used it was in *Laurel Canyon* [2002], where I felt the freest sexually. I found that I could most easily project comfortable sexuality by doing the male types of things. I'd watch the young guys I was working with, and adopted their gestures and relationship to their bodies — jeans, legs wide apart, knees crossed, louche bodies. *Laurel Canyon* was my older woman/younger man movie — it's a threshold for actresses. But, of course, after it I started getting more scripts for 'the older woman,' and I said, 'I've done that, I don't want to do that again.'"

It was interesting to have this conversation over lunch at Fairway, the big, unpretentious neighborhood grocery store on Manhattan's Upper West Side. The contrast between our topic and her down-to-earth, unglamorous presentation was stark. "It's your job to be vain in my business," she said, sitting there without a speck of makeup, "and we actually call the hair and the makeup people 'the vanities,' even though not much can really be done with hair and makeup. The antiaging magic has to come from *lighting*."

As an aside, Nora Ephron has joked to me over the years that if we could mount little lights on an apparatus in front of our faces that would illuminate us artfully, then we wouldn't need to do half the cosmetic stuff we do.

Frances McDormand said that she used to dye her hair darker. "I had a thing about not being blond—I wanted to promote this tough, brunette, intellectual thing. But the really dark hair didn't match when the wrinkles started coming in." She's hopeful about her professional options as she ages (she's forty-eight). "With my gray hair—and I'm just starting to get my grays, and I love them—I'm going to get jobs. I think gray hair at twenty-five is different. I don't think I could have gotten work with gray hair at twenty-five, but I think I will now."

I asked my friend Mark, a successful screenwriter who's over fifty, about the double standard for men in Hollywood. "Men have always had a different perch in terms of vanity and the duration of their careers. And call it sexism or wish fulfillment on the part of aging studio executives, but Hollywood has never had a problem casting older men with much younger women. One of the great stories of Hollywood was Cary Grant insisting that this [age difference] not go unremarked in the film *Charade*. It's a great movie, made more so by Grant [fifty-nine at the time] telling Audrey Hepburn [thirty-four] that he's old enough to be her father. He wasn't afraid of his age. But then, of course, he didn't have to be—he was Cary Grant. And in another example of this, Sean Connery [sixty-nine at the time] apparently insisted on the same thing in the 1999 film *Entrapment*, which costarred Catherine Zeta-Jones [thirty]. But then again, he is Sean Connery."

But the "ageism" in Hollywood goes beyond on-camera

looks—and even extends to people who don't perform. "You hear a lot about writers 'aging out,'" Mark says, "along with studio executives, agents, and directors. You really can't kid anyone about your age. You can dye your hair"—he says he doesn't, although it's still completely brown—"and you can have all the plastic surgery you want until you look ridiculous, like morning talk show hosts who've had so much work done they almost look like they've been a burn victim, but in the end, a lot of it's about your outlook, your mind-set.

"You simply can't walk into a room complaining that movies aren't as good as they used to be, or that 'kids today know nothing.' It tags you as being out of touch the same way you'd be out of touch if you said you didn't use e-mail, or you didn't understand or weren't interested in things like MySpace.com or blogging. As a writer or director out here, it's your job to stay current and youthful. You may not like video games, but you'd better know about them and recognize their importance. You may not agree with the way movies are cut these days, but you'd better recognize that this is a cinematic grammar and syntax that the audience understands.

"But it isn't easy," Mark added. "And sometimes you feel that just when you're finally mastering all this [as a craftsperson], your experience is devalued. And I've experienced this—recently, a young executive replaced me on a project for almost no reason, other than what my lawyer explained to me. 'He's a thirty-two-year-old, and he'd rather hang out with another thirty-two-year-old.'

"Can you *legitimately* 'age out'? Of course. Should a forty-five-year-old be trying to write college comedies, or a fifty-eight-year-old, I'm-having-problems-meeting-girls films? Absolutely not. But just look at Clint Eastwood: he's always acted his age, always dealt with stories as an actor that were appropriate for his age, and never shied away from who he was. And he's always worked."

So, in the cases of Cary Grant and Sean Connery and Clint Eastwood, their archetypal sexiness as they grew older gave them the confidence to be frank about their age, but that frankness — that basic sense of authenticity they conveyed — made them seem even sexier. Can't this work for women as well, on-screen and in real life?

Throughout my scores of interviews for this book, almost to a person, interviewees cited "the media" as the drivers of Americans' new, turbocharged obsession with looking young. But Mark, the screenwriter, zeroed in on what sector of the media he blames. "If I were going to pinpoint who's more responsible for the plastic-surgery craze, I'd point more to Barbara Walters than I would to Hollywood. We've never really pretended that our Hollywood version of the girl next door was *actually* the girl next door. For me, it was the woman who was in your house every day: the *newscasters,* those women" — who aren't supposed to be human confections playing roles but serious, real people telling us the plain truth — "not actresses, who changed things." Again, ironically, the feminist victories in the workplace in the '70s and '80s put women in TV news but also had the unintended effect of making every kind of artificial youth more acceptable and even obligatory.

The issue of youth and professional livelihood came into national prominence in the mid-'80s when Christine Craft, a reporter for the ABC affiliate in Kansas City, became a poster girl for age discrimination. Her boss actually told her that she was, at thirty-nine, "too old, too unattractive, and not deferential enough to men," and demoted her. Craft filed a breach of contract lawsuit and was awarded $500,000 in damages.

One would think that with the graying of the boomer generation, the issue of age discrimination in television would dissipate, but in 2005 the *Wall Street Journal* ran a story on the case of Marny Stanier Midkiff, who had worked at the Weather Channel for sixteen years as both an on-air reporter and a behind-the-scenes supervisor. She was fired in 2003 at age forty-one, she claims in a lawsuit, because the channel systematically "wanted to get rid of on-air talent over forty in favor of younger meteorologists." Her lawyer, according to the *Wall Street Journal*, "claims the channel has spent the past two years going after a 'sexier look' and wanted 'top buttons open in the blouse.'" They "hired an image consultant to help female anchors appear younger and sexier."

I asked Emmylou Harris what it had been like to grow visibly, unquestionably older in front of millions of people. "It's difficult being in the public eye because people are always comparing you to album covers and films and to how you looked in your twenties. Everywhere you go, there's a video camera and camera phones, and we now live in a very voyeuristic society. There's rarely a moment when you feel you're alone.

"But I'm lucky—I'm a folksinger, so in a sense we *start* old. We're singing about universal issues that are timeless, and that lets one grow old gracefully. Unlike rock music, which is about more overtly sexual things, the majority of my material is timeless. As a folksinger, if your voice is still there, your audience is not expecting you to act forever young. It's a continuum." She says she's had a great role model in her eighty-six-year-old mother, whose natural strawberry-blond hair has turned a different shade of gray from her own. "My mother looks her age but transcends it.

"I don't think vanity is a bad thing. Looking good is important. But we need to *think* about what we want to look like at fifty, sixty, or eighty." She says she never intended to have her hair become part of her public persona, "but it just is. I think my hair lets people think that they have an option."

One wonders why more women haven't adopted Emmylou Harris's or Steve Martin's approach. Jeff, the Hollywood television writer, is a friend of Martin's. "Steve is the bravest man in show-business history," he told me, exaggerating in his customary way, "because he was going gray very quickly in his twenties and chose to do absolutely nothing about it. The huge long-term advantage for the Steve Martin approach is that he was white-haired in his thirties and is white-haired in his sixties and thus appears to have barley aged at all." I think it's a brilliant strategy, and one, frankly, that I hope will work for me, even though I'm not a celebrity and was a couple of decades late to the party.

Red, White, and Blue, but Seldom Gray

I ASSUMED THAT while it was a challenge to find unapologetically older women in show business, it would be a slam dunk to find gray-haired women in politics, one of the few professional arenas in which maturity and seasoning should be salient requirements. But I couldn't have been more wrong.

I got a copy of the 109th Congress Congressional Directory for 2005–2006. The directory has photographs of each of the senators and the members of the House of Representatives. Of the fourteen female senators, who range in age from forty-seven to seventy-four, *not a single one has gray hair.* Of the sixty-seven female members of the House, the youngest of whom is thirty-seven, only six have gray hair, half Republicans and half Democrats. All of them, interestingly, are from just four states—California, New York, Pennsylvania, and North Carolina.

To my eye, the men in Congress who most obviously color

their hair look particularly ridiculous—and the women who plainly *don't* dye look honest and straightforward, as if they probably spend their time and energy on what's important to their constituents and the country. So why don't more women in politics relax a little bit and show their true color, particularly when they get lambasted in the press for their youth-preserving efforts? Earlier this year, Ted Olson, the former solicitor general and Republican lawyer, chose to make Botox jokes about the two most prominent women in Congress, the new Speaker of the House, Nancy Pelosi, and Hillary Clinton. Congress could amuse itself, Olson said, by "searching for any sign of movement in Speaker Pelosi's forehead," while the Senate would be entertained by the "expressionless, Pelosi-like forehead of Senator Clinton."

Searching Yahoo for "Hillary Clinton" and "hair," I found that a shocking 3,270,000 hits came up, and a huge fraction discussed how her style did or did not matter to her politically. Hillary herself raised the issue in her 2001 speech at Yale's commencement—in which she good-naturedly warned the graduates that "hair matters." Clinton decided not to wear the traditional mortarboard because "hats do a real number on your hair." In 2002 she joked with a *New York Times* reporter that the title for her memoir could have been *Headbands and Headaches.*

RadarOnline.com ran a piece about the "eight worst trends in congressional coifs" just before 2006's midterm elections. "In the end," it said, "the pivotal decisions Americans face may all come down to hair." The article quoted a political image consultant named Sherry Maysonave, president of Empowerment Enterprises: "It's one of the first things voters notice. Hair is a strong indicator of a candidate's position and politics."

But not all the expert opinion is disheartening. In the '90s, political scientists Shawn Rosenberg, Shulamit Kahn, Thuy Tran, and Minh-Thu Le published a study called "Creating a Political Image: Shaping Appearance and Manipulating the Vote." Their methodology was not unlike that which I'd used in my survey—showing people photographs of different women, claiming they were candidates for office, and asking, in a fake election that the respondents thought was real, whom they'd be inclined to vote for. Simply by changing the women's makeup, styling, and attire, "in two of the three elections, enhancing the image of one candidate while diminishing the image of the other reversed the final outcome." "Enhancing" in this instance meant utilizing more conservative clothes and shorter hair. But while the researchers discovered, not surprisingly, that image affects voter preferences, they also found that "physical attractiveness does *not* affect political image"—and that "generally, women who appeared to be older were evaluated more positively."

Beyond the Beltway, it seems, authenticity is more permissible. Of the eight female state governors as of 2006, three had gray hair, all Democrats. During last year's elections, my friend Joel Stein, the *Los Angeles Times* columnist, sent me an e-mail—the subject line: "More hot gray-haired ladies"—with a photograph of Montana state legislator Denise Moore, a forty-nine-year-old Republican with long silver hair.

I sought firsthand insight from someone who'd been in the

fray out in Middle America—Ann Richards, the former governor of Texas, who died some months after we spoke. Her hair was indelibly linked to her persona. Her obituary in the *New York Times* last fall began, "Ann W. Richards, the silver-haired Texas activist…"

Over an extremely candid lunch, during which we shared intimacies about our respective struggles with alcohol, parenting, and weight, Richards was equally frank about the unfortunate ways in which image, particularly the televised image, constricts the range of women deemed to be electable candidates for public office.

"I don't not dye my hair out of vanity," she said. "I just don't do it." She became governor at fifty-seven. "The news media talked about my hair—no one else. I never found my hair to be an issue. And anyone who cared about my hair wanted to talk about how *big* it was, so being white-haired got lost in the big-hair [discussion]. People would say, 'I'm for the woman with the big white hair,' and not care a whit. There's a saying in Texas that women have big hair to match their rear ends. Now that my rear end is smaller, so is my hair."

Richards suggested that this obsession with the way people look is a result of the reality that "we've bought into a fake society when you accept as fact that women who do nothing but pose for photographs and stand around at parties are beautiful. I mean, that's not what I think of as beauty."

But she was also clear-eyed enough to understand that markers of youthfulness, like it or not, are important in politics. "The television image has become so powerfully important. Politicians need to have a constancy of image. You can't appear to be too flashy because it will send the wrong message, but at the same time you need to appear to be energetic. Just watch how a politician walks across a stage or up stairs — it's bouncy, and they need to appear to have all of the energy in the world even if they're older. This whole business of trying to look younger than you really are has something to do with a culture that has convinced itself that looking young is a valuable asset.

"Washington is more image-conscious than anyplace I know," Governor Richards told me. "Consultants convey to clients what has worked [in the past], which definitely narrows the range of what people will do. So everyone ends up mirroring what successfully elected people have done before." But that doesn't allow for any natural personality quirk to peek through.

"I've been with a lot of women in a lot of races, and the women face lots of difficult things. If they are too young-looking, they have to worry about looking inexperienced, or if they are too old, they'll seem tired. When I was losing to Bush [in Texas] in 1994, I had a very good friend who wrote me a long and sweet letter and said I had to get a face-lift. 'With the opportunities you have, it'll help — everybody is getting them.' She was well-intentioned, but I've got better things to do with my time. Women running for office worry that if they're single, their opponent will claim that they are a lesbian — I don't know anyone who's escaped that one. You can't run and look too floozyish. It's better to be boring than to be jazzy-looking.

"The issue is much more significant for women because the hurdle is higher in our society. We're not sure what we want our elected officials to be—mother, mistress, or caretaker. But the electorate knows it when they see it."

An acquaintance of mine who's a member of a female senator's staff summed up Washington for me. "Politics," she said, "is a business where you can be very old and even feeble and maintain hero status. Just look at [Senator Robert] Byrd and his almost ninety years. He trembles from some disorder, has bright white hair, and wears the most ghastly clothes imaginable. Barbara Bush is another totally different example—her openness with white hair and being older is a plus. I do think *women* in politics and power are judged much more, and thus unfairly, when it comes to looks. Just take a look at any political article or profile of a woman pol and see how immediately what they are wearing, from makeup to clothes, is brought up—Condi, Hillary, and most other women in that spotlight all have adjusted accordingly. But my guess is they have to be much more careful to avoid artificial fixes that stand out." Take, for example, Jeanine Pirro—the failed Republican U.S. Senate and New York state attorney general candidate. "Her appearance of plastic surgery certainly did not help her."

In October 2006, just weeks before the midterm elections, John Spencer, the Republican candidate for senator from New York, made a public crack about the appearance of his opponent to a reporter for the *New York Daily News.* Spencer said that Hillary Clinton had evolved from an ugly duckling to a presentable fifty-nine-year-old woman with the help of "millions of dollars" of "work." In the wake of that story, the *New York Times* found a plastic surgeon named Dr. Cap Lesesne who said he had done work on eighteen federal, state, and local officials: "Politicians want to come away looking younger, better, healthier, but with something that does not say they have had plastic surgery."

As we were saying good-bye on the street, Ann Richards concluded our conversation with the following thought—which so inspired me that I spontaneously hugged her. "I think wisdom and age have value," she said, "and it's really important, and if all we do is continue this whole business of focusing on youth, we'll miss that all ages can be wonderful, not only personally, but the culture will miss that ingredient as well. And I think that if we make improvements on this score in subsequent generations, I believe my grandchildren may not be alcoholics." I understood the leap she was making, and I absolutely agreed. Different order of magnitude, sure, but maybe if I reject the obligatory hair coloring that my grandmother and mother embraced, my own daughters will have greater leeway in how they can present themselves as they mature.

Nine to Five

BUT DOES A REGULAR professional woman of forty-five or fifty-five have to worry as much about her appearance and looking her age as do actresses and politicians? I would like to say no, of course, that in the real world signs of normal aging are acceptable, that doing the job well is what really counts, and that a middle-aged entrepreneur or manager needn't worry about the cultural pressures to look younger. You and I are not Cameron Diaz. We are not selling sex appeal.

Alas, I discovered, in many professional worlds, gray hair is a real liability. Our laws and, more and more, our cultural norms have made bias against older people and women unacceptable, but at the same time a great, sad, silly loophole has been opened up in our new, ostensibly equal society: it seems that discrimination against gray-haired women is very real. An employer might never admit that he (or she) is more inclined to hire or promote a man over a woman, or a young person over an older one...but a brunette or blonde or redhead over a woman with gray or white hair? Consciously or unconsciously, *yes,* absolutely.

Women worry more than they should about how gray hair might negatively affect their romantic and sexual opportunities. But how we choose to package ourselves to achieve professional credibility and success is a more difficult challenge.

Context counts: a high-tech business or sales job is different from engineering or academics. So does the cultural geography (LA versus Minneapolis, Dallas versus Boston); the organizational level (chief financial officer versus assistant talent agent); and the median age of people in the organization or profession. Each determines the image a woman will be pressured to adopt, and how strongly. Is competence or creativity the most important attribute to convey? And what signifiers are used to "read" those qualities? Would a woman with spiky orange hair land a COO job? Would someone who looks like Meg Whitman of eBay get the gig as head of a record label? Is it more advantageous to blend into the corporate milieu or to stand out?

Consider, for instance, the portraits of the women who attended the 2005 *Fortune* magazine conference for the 50 Most Powerful Women in Business. Of the 324 women — CEOs, CFOs, and other executives from the areas of packaged goods, banking, entertainment, government, defense, and law (with an average age of about forty-seven) — exactly 11, or 3.4 percent, had discernible gray hair. At any comparable gathering of men, nearly half the attendees would be gray. And most of the senior gray- and white-haired female executives whom I asked to interview about their hair declined. "I don't want to be known as the 'woman on Wall Street with white hair,'" said one.

I know that a reason I felt (relatively) comfortable deciding to let my hair color go natural is that I'm now self-employed. My professional success is no longer very closely linked to how I dress or style my hair.

A decade ago, I was the executive vice president and worldwide creative director for MTV Networks' Nickelodeon and Nick at Nite, working in one of the loosest major-corporate environments imaginable. But in addition to the brand-managing creative-director position, I also had line responsibility—budgets, manufacturing, sales, and marketing—for Nickelodeon's nontelevision businesses, such as toys and publishing and music, and thus had to present to my Viacom corporate overlords an image of a person who could responsibly run a multimillion-dollar enterprise. Those of us who ran business segments that obliged us to deal with outside partners all wore suits with either pants or skirts, while those responsible for programming and the more purely creative output of the company were far, far more casual in their attire. I straddled both realms—I looked like a "suit," but since I laughed and spoke frankly and freely cursed (the last vestige of rebellion, a quarter-century later, against my very proper mother and the nuns at my convent school), I also was able to appear as a "creative" when necessary. As Matthew Perry, playing the head writer on NBC's *Studio 60* last year, said to

Amanda Peet, the head of the fictional network, "You look like one of them but talk like one of us."

Underlying the business-versus-creative aspect of deciphering the corporate dress code at MTV Networks was one nonnegotiable quality: no matter what kind of work you did, it was essential to come across as youthful. I am convinced that one senior-executive colleague of mine at MTV never achieved his full potential because he simply looked too much like a conservative banker — the victim of a different kind of modern glass ceiling that screens executives on the basis of perceived sensibility rather than gender.

Just as Mick Jagger (sixty-four) and Paul McCartney (sixty-five) believe they have to remain frozen in a circa-1970s groovy-guy look, so, too, do the executives who operate businesses that sell music and TV and movies to people of their grandchildren's generation. I'd guess that close to half the male executives with whom I worked in the entertainment industry — who now range from their forties to early sixties — dye their hair. When it comes to hair color and holding on for dear life to a slight illusion of youthfulness, they are nearly as fear-driven and tyrannized as women.

And this is not a phenomenon unique to a company like MTV Networks, focused on programming for teenagers and twentysomethings. People of all ages buy and use digital technology, but the Internet and software and consumer-electronics industries are dominated by people under forty. According to

Techies.com, the average age of a software developer in Silicon Valley is twenty-four. A study conducted by the National Academy of Sciences found that older workers in the technology sector are three times more likely to lose their jobs in layoffs than are younger workers. And according to a survey by *Network World* magazine, only 13 percent of tech managers who are thirty or younger had hired anyone over forty during the previous year. Job descriptions in the sector include language like "energetic," "flexible thinkers," "fast-paced"…code words, of course, for "young." And, as a practical matter, for "non-gray-haired."

I decided to investigate if my gray hair would be a disadvantage if I were to reenter business. So I proceeded to my next round of real-world fibbing and made appointments with headhunters.

One of them, Ann Carlsen, a recruiter in telecommunications and technology who was based in Boulder, Colorado, was bracingly blunt. She told me that if I was serious about reentering the corporate workforce after a ten-year hiatus, I would have to be prepared for a long and frustrating process. "At your age," she said, ravaging my (simulated) hopes for full-time reentry into business, "you should be a consultant." In other words, according to Carlsen, I'm over.

I asked her if she saw any basic differences in the kinds of candidates that different industries look for. "Across the board, more companies are targeting younger demos, so they are focusing on wanting to hire people whom they believe will think like the animal. This is happening in all disciplines at the VP level and above." She said that "corporate fit" is more important in hiring than actual skills. Clients won't tell her straight out, of course, that one of her potential hires didn't get a particular job because he or she was too old. "Instead, they'll say that the person just 'wasn't a good fit for the culture,'" or that the "person is 'overqualified.'" Of course, "overqualified" can have real meaning—someone who'll be unhappy with the lack of challenge or authority—but it can also be code for a younger manager who is uncomfortable at the prospect of bossing someone older.

I asked Ann if she could remember any specific case where someone she headhunted didn't get a job because he or she had gray hair. Sure, she said matter-of-factly, "I just had one last week. Two women and one man presented," meaning went in to interview with the potential employer. "One of the women, fifty-four, wore a nice suit, but she didn't have a cool, fresh look. When we debriefed, the client said, 'I loved her and loved her personality, but she wouldn't be a good fit.'" Carlsen had no doubt that the main reason her candidate didn't get the job was her gray hair.

Ann says she doesn't coach candidates on appearance before a job interview. She thinks that it's important for the client to have a sense of the real candidate. However, if someone has been rejected a few times, they "tend to figure it out themselves. Across the board they will color their hair if they get turned down." I asked her if she thought women's appearances were judged more harshly than men's. *Duh.* "The deck is even more stacked against older women. You've got to look like you've been working out. You need good shoes and accessories, and the tan. The men [who run companies] tend to dismiss older women as not relevant. If the job is in sales or any area with high visibility, the issue is further compounded. If you put two women up for the same sales job and one is blond and hip and the other more dowdy, there is never a doubt about how that will come out, regardless of the position or the company or the skill set."

There are also striking, stereotypical regional differences, she said. In California companies, "people over forty are out to pasture."

I asked Carlsen her age and whether or not she dyed her hair. "I'm fifty," she said, "and I get my roots done every three weeks." Carlsen also confirmed that among her roughly one hundred employer clients, for whom she conducts more than one hundred fifty searches a year, there is not a single woman with gray hair.

Pat Mastandrea, the former COO of the British satellite channel Sky TV, is now head of the Cheyenne Group, a New York–based executive-recruitment firm that specializes in placing C-level candidates (CEO, CFO, COO) in media, entertainment, and education companies. She doesn't have a single female client *or* candidate with gray hair. Mastandrea thought the degree of pressure to look young was more a function of the particular job than the industry. "But I would say in certain businesses it *is* important. I had a candidate who was in sales, and one day she just woke up and looked around and realized that all of her colleagues were in their thirties, and her clients were in their twenties, and she was in her fifties, and she realized that there was a disconnect and she had to change fields. Sales positions are not as accepting of the aging process."

I asked Mastandrea if she had witnessed overt age discrimination. "Some clients aren't even aware of their aversions or know why they discriminate," she said. I think this is exactly right, and a main reason why discriminatory "hair-colorism," if you will, is so entrenched and pervasive. "They couldn't begin to articulate why [they think] someone wouldn't be a 'good fit.'"

The month the feature about my hair appeared in *More,* Peggy Northrop, the fifty-three-year-old editor in chief, wrote frankly in her editor's letter about giving in to the pressure to dye her own hair as she got older.

A friend in Washington, DC, once told me cheerfully, "Women who are interested in power dye their hair." I was in my midthirties and already completely gray, but because I looked thirtyish (except for the hair)...I opted to stay silver. Wearing my hair short and spiky, and with funky eyeglasses and red lipstick, I felt fine—even, dare I say, cool. Then I turned forty-five and was passed over for a job I really wanted. I blamed the hair. Given that I suddenly had wrinkles to go with my gray hair and that I was about to hunt for a new job, I took the logical next step. Hello, high-maintenance highlights; good-bye, thousands of dollars. Aging confidently isn't easy in a culture where "new" and "cool" still usually equal "young."

If the woman responsible for creating the serious modern glossy magazine for and about women in their forties and fifties and sixties feels compelled to succumb to the unspoken pressures, then clearly our fears that gray hair might limit our professional opportunities are not silly or misplaced—sad and wrong, maybe, but not unfounded. Perception becomes reality.

But a brave few women flout the taboo on gray hair in the executive suite, even in the youth-obsessed entertainment industry, such as, most spectacularly, Lauren Zalaznick, a former executive at VH1 and now president of NBC Universal Cable's network Bravo. She's forty-three and completely gray. And she turned out to be more than a no-BS, compulsively candid person about the unusual way she looks. When I asked her if she'd be willing to talk on the record about this fraught subject, she leaped at the chance.

Speaking on whether a gray-haired person chooses to color her hair, she said, "There is no more transparent test of authenticity. Hair maintenance in every other realm is one of *removal*—waxing, lasering, and bleaching. Boob jobs are still seen through layers of clothing," which muddles the issue. "Surgery is not widely noticed and certainly not openly discussed." Gray hair in the "workplace is *the* point of male-female difference more than any others, in terms of de rigueur workplace fashion. I am almost always the youngest but by far the grayest [woman] at any boardroom or ballroom function."

I asked Lauren if she thought her hair color had had any particular impact on her professional life. She thought for a bit and then said that she believed there was a "higher barrier to goodwill if you don't act and look a certain way at work—but there is also a very high barrier to breaking out of mediocrity in any area of one's own life. Very few people take risks, but people who make choices outside of the norms do get further emotionally and materially when it pays off."

I'd assumed that working for a button-down corporate parent such as General Electric would be different than working for MTV Networks, my former parent company, which operates VH1. But she claimed counterintuitively that conservative GE was, in fact, *more* tolerant of diversity of style. "At NBC many obvious things are true," she said. "There is wider tolerance for short, bald, non-good-looking men than there is for heavy, gray-haired women." Lauren, in fact, is quite slim. "But the evidence is there [at NBC that] if you can contribute, and in all those subtle workplace ways not directly affront people's sensibility of the norm, then your work can speak louder than your look.

"On the other hand," she added, "my gray hair is just one more example of how poorly I fit into corporate life." She told me about a New York–based colleague who had been promoted to a new West Coast position. "And all of a sudden this formerly New York lady had blond hair and had a lot of [surgical] work done. I guess you just make that decision that if you're willing to move to LA, then you also say to yourself, 'My moving expenses include the complete makeover.' It's totally normal in this business."

Does her gray make her "memorable" in an advantageous way? "I don't think I've gone so far as to cultivate a look like Brian Grazer"—the Hollywood producer with spiky black hair—"but it's almost like I just don't think I'm successful when I do try to fit in." Zalaznick is who she is, and does her work, damn the torpedoes. And, of course, doesn't have a single female colleague with gray hair.

Ellen Levine, sixty-four, is editorial director at Hearst Magazines, where she's worked since 1994. Her long hair has been white since she was in her thirties, and Levine notes that Hearst is unique in having several gray- and white-haired female executives—"the head of personnel, the head of communications, one of our senior marketing people. It's a little bit of a club, and we kind of high-five each other." Hearst is headquartered in New York. "I do believe that gray hair is accepted better in some parts of the country than in others. In LA," she said, before I'd mentioned my trip there as a gray-haired newbie, "*no one* has gray hair. When I'm out there, I get a sense that they caricature a woman with gray hair as a person with fuddy-duddy, square-shaped, cropped hair; a matronly suit; and a stodgy but safe automobile."

Levine was recently headhunted to be on a corporate board and thought her white hair was actually an advantage, because it connoted a sense of comfort and authority. The phrase "eminence grise," after all, is French for "gray eminence," shorthand for "age equaling wisdom and good judgment."

She also thinks it's possible that the dubiousness of corporate headhunters about gray hair that I encountered may have been a rationalization for laziness. "They are in the business of trying to sell people, so they may not try too hard to sell someone whom they perceive might be a little different and harder to place." I told her that the headhunters I'd talked with were all women. "Well, women are their own worst critics."

Anna Quindlen has a few gray strands in her hair and has no intention of dyeing it. She spent the first half of her career as a star reporter and columnist for the *New York Times*. "I was always the wunderkind. I embraced aging differently from how I might have in another profession. I always equated gray hair with gravitas, and I worried that people felt that I lacked that. And my husband, Gerry, a lawyer, didn't get a job one time because the client wanted someone with a 'little more snow on the roof.'"

I was frankly surprised by my research. I had expected the outcome of my investigation to be that gray hair would make it far more difficult for women to date but that it wouldn't really have much direct bearing on employment. And the women in my national survey shared that supposition: 35 percent admitted they were "very" or "somewhat" worried about gray hair making them unsexy, whereas only 19 percent worried as much about gray hair blunting their "career edge." But the real-world truth seems to be exactly the opposite, at least outside the professions—medicine, law, the academy—and not-for-profit worlds. Women face diminished professional opportunity if they have gray hair. There seems to be real job discrimination, and of a kind that no law—the Gray Hair Equal Opportunity Act of 2009?—can reasonably remedy. Some women can turn their gray hair into an asset, but the gumption necessary to pull that off—courage, even—is high.

It's Not the Gray, It's the Clothes

I WONDERED WHAT IMAGE consultants would tell me about my prospects if I proposed—that is, pretended to propose— reentering the executive world as a woman with gray hair. (And, by the way, what does it say about our society that "image consultancy" is a profession? My mother missed her true calling.) Unlike the corporate recruiters, who need to think about their long-term relationships with their clients and my actual experience and skills, the image consultants' focus would be purely and unapologetically on my packaging.

As a somewhat credulous person, I'd met with more than my fair share of New Age therapists and psychics and alternative-medicine practitioners over the years who'd left me wondering about their qualifications. And while I wasn't suggesting that image consulting was any more snake-oil salesmanship than most other consulting businesses, I wanted to make certain that I met with firms that had whatever kind of accreditation was available. The Association of Image Consultants International is the go-to source for journalists writing about the field, so I decided to use their membership as my guide for appointments. Because I lived in New York, there were, not surprisingly, a considerable number of potential firms to choose from. I decided to meet with three, each from distinctly different parts of Manhattan: one on the Upper East Side, the city's old-school neighborhood of bankers, Wall Street types, and rich ladies who lunch; a second firm on the Upper West Side, a neighborhood of old-time liberals, professionals, and journalists; and another in lower Manhattan, in the Flatiron District, a part of town where advertising, design, and media firms predominate.

The Web site for the Upper East Side place proclaimed, needlessly, "First impressions matter," and went on to promise that I'd end up with a "personal transformation" and a "lifelong understanding" of how style could add to my personal power.

Heady stuff. Sign me up.

Before going to my first, $250 session, I was required to fill out a questionnaire—not just about age, weight, and hair color but also about my sense of identity and whether I thought other people found me attractive. I was hesitant about giving out that kind of intimate information to an organization that I'd discovered online. I filled out the questionnaire, trying to provide the minimum and most neutral information possible yet still seem like a credible potential client. I also chose to go to the appointment dressed in a way that gave as few visual cues as possible about what kind of person I might be: a simple A-line black skirt, unadorned black cashmere sweater, flat black boots and tights—in other words, a generic New Yorker's uniform.

It was a bleak winter day when I arrived at the company's address, a nondescript 1970s high-rise in the East 80s—a residential building. I found it weird that I was showing up at someone's apartment. But maybe this was how image consulting worked. So into the apartment I went.

I was welcomed by a woman in her thirties, Ginger, who wore a leopard-print cashmere sweater with caribou feathers trimming the deep V-neck and cuffs, slim black wool pants, and black suede Manolo Blahnik stiletto boots—an outfit that would have been less surprising to me if I'd made an appointment with a dominatrix. Not only did we have dramatically different styles but my consulting diva also had a serious cold—and I'm only a couple of notches down from Howard Hughes in the germ-phobia department.

I told Ginger that I was thinking about returning to a corporate gig after almost a decade of self-employment, and since I felt I might be out of touch, I wanted advice on how I should present myself. Within minutes, it was clear to me that she had not even glanced at my careful answers to her questionnaire—she didn't once refer to any of my written comments. We were clearly getting off on the wrong foot.

Ginger seemed bored by my non-feather-encrusted persona and acted as if it were a burden for her to take my $250. Her way of getting into a discussion about how to "change" my look was by pulling out a book published by *In Style* magazine. She summoned her energy enough to suggest that I'd look better in V-neck tops than turtlenecks because turtlenecks shorten your neck and "just shouldn't be worn." I was at that moment wearing a mock turtleneck. Perhaps she thought I needed tough love. She also thought I should wear flat-front, straight-legged pants. Okay, fine. But not *exactly* advice based on who I was and leading to a personal transformation that would add to a lifelong understanding of my personal power.

Finally, I asked whether she thought I should do anything to my hair—did she think the gray might put off prospective bosses? The only doubt I had about her answer was which shade of blond she would recommend.

"*No,* leave it as it is," she said, shocking me. She thought my hair color was striking and that if I should do anything at all, it should be to *accentuate* the white and make the cut chunkier. "Even if you dyed your hair black, it wouldn't make you look twenty-five. I'm here to help make people feel more comfortable in their own skin, not to reinvent them. I'm just someone with a fresh eye who can help you accentuate your best features." I had set the whole meeting up on the assumption that an image consultant would tell me to color my hair if I wanted to be viable in the job market, and I was stunned by this young woman's feedback. And because Ginger was so clearly uninterested in me, I found myself believing her candor about my hair.

Talking about hair seemed to perk Ginger up, and even

though she'd informed me that her company didn't recommend particular hair and makeup styles, she proceeded to tell me exactly what I should do. "Put a little white pencil under your eyes, do just the corners of your eyes with mascara, and use NARS Red Lizard lipstick." A makeup branded "Lizard"? *If you say so . . .* She also suggested that I adopt the pale color palette of Carmen — "You know, the white-haired model?" — and that I try Pilates to stay in shape. And then, $250 poorer, I found that my session was over.

Needless to say, I was a bit gun-shy for my second appointment, this one with Lauren Solomon of LS Image, Inc., on the Upper West Side. When I phoned her to ask about the details of her process, she told me that there was no magical system to this and that she worked by trying to find out where I was in my life and where I wanted to go. Once again I told her that I was interested in returning to the job market after a ten-year hiatus raising my kids. Her rate of $500 for an initial two-hour consultation blew even my New Yorker's numbed-to-ridiculous-expense-for-unnecessary-service mind. But I was also deeply curious about what $500 would buy me.

We arranged to meet midmorning at an upscale sandwich restaurant in her neighborhood; at least I wasn't going to her apartment. I arrived and realized that we had failed to tell each other what we looked like, so I called her cell phone to tell her where I'd be sitting. "Great, I'll be there in ten minutes," she said, "and you can't miss me. I'll be the one in the gold leather jacket." *Oh,*

God, I thought, *how can I possibly expect to have any useful insight from someone wearing a gold jacket at ten in the morning?* I was now anticipating another Ginger experience.

This time I'd broken out of the New Yorker's black uniform and worn navy blue corduroys, a white shirt, a gray sweater, and my trusty gray suede Merrell shoes. The forty-six-year-old Solomon rushed up and took in my whole just-in-from-the-countryside look in one quick, jaundiced glance. This time she was the one dressed in black. Her only color accent was a dark ruby-reddish strand of glittery beads wrapped around her neck—in my mind an accessory better suited to evening wear, but then again I wouldn't don a gold leather jacket either. Her hair was dyed a very dark brown.

The first thing she did was pass me two xeroxed "Self-Perception" questionnaires and ask me to fill them out while she got coffee. I was required to use three words to describe myself, three words to describe how others perceived me, and three words to describe how I'd like others to perceive me. The three words I used to describe myself were: "confident," "competitive," and "loyal." What others thought: "confident," "generous," and "helpful." And what I wanted others to think: "creative," "fun," and "passionate."

Solomon immediately zeroed in on the inherent disconnect—"confident" and "creative" could go together, but my hopes of what others might see in me seemed at odds, given my matronly suburbanite attire. She asked what I'd done before taking time off, and when I said I'd worked at MTV Networks, she basically did a double take. I asked her why. "Your shoes, they just don't fit with someone who'd work at MTV." *Wow!* She was fast — my feet had been under the table when she'd arrived, and I had no idea she'd even seen my Merrells. Although her conclusion seemed knee-jerk, I also considered that maybe my visual assessment of her was equally so.

I asked her about her work. "I've found that if the image of a person doesn't go with what they are saying, then I have to work much harder to really hear what they are saying." *Touché,* I thought. I had to get over my bias about her outfit to see if what she had to say was helpful. "My job," she went on, "is to help people have the outside fit what the inside is saying. People need to represent their message." She told me that she'd started helping friends prepare for job interviews while she was in business school and then began to do more of that as a sideline when she was working in commercial banking. She proudly told of two of her colleagues at the bank who had had all of the requisite skills for advancement but kept being passed over for promotion and how she'd helped them. The first, an overweight woman with the beginnings of gray hair, she made over — getting her new slimming clothing and dyeing the gray streaks.

"Guess what? She began to get the promotions!" Solomon did something similar for the male colleague, with comparable results, and realized that she was onto something.

THE STORY ABOUT her first client — how coloring over gray had helped her friend break out of a professional rut — made me realize that my charade of wanting to go back to a corporate job would prevent me from getting the benefit of Solomon's insights into what really goes on in the hiring and promotion of her clients. I told her what I was up to.

"I knew something was up," she said. "You just seemed too vague."

Now we could really get down to business. And I think that maybe this experience was yet another metaphor for how a false hair color might get in the way of people having more direct, productive interactions. The more we tell the truth in the way we look, maybe, the more we're inclined to tell the truth in other ways, and thus encourage other people to be honest with us.

Solomon had a broad spectrum of clients, ranging from those in financial services (accounting, insurance, investment, banking), to packaged goods (Pfizer), to nonprofits (AARP), to entertainment, to law, and even advised other professional coaches. She told me that she felt women could get away with gray hair in the service professions if *every single other aspect* of their presentation was perfectly styled. In those businesses, she said, "you don't get a 'bad hair day.'" She also asserted that she believed professionals in those fields actually gained credibility if they looked like they'd had enough life experience to be able to advise a client well. "I've had clients in those fields who actually looked too young and to whom I've given glasses and, yes, even in one case, colored their hair [gray] to look older and more mature."

Unlike the headhunters with whom I'd spoken, Solomon claimed that about 50 percent of both genders of her clients were gray. According to her, these clients almost always had a shade of gray to which high- and lowlights—artificial streaks of dark gray or silver—had been added to give the hair color some "dimension," but nonetheless, the overall effect was one of gray hair. I wondered if she could describe any instances of clients not getting jobs or promotions because of gray hair.

"Oh, yes. I had a salt-and-pepper client who had been at the same publishing house for years and was told at her exit interview that she'd been fired because she seemed 'too conservative overall.' That woman believed that letting her hair be naturally gray as she had aged had been a huge, although unspoken, part of management's 'conservative' assessment." She said that the publishing house had just not seen the gray-haired woman "in the boardroom." The client kept her gray hair and went to work successfully for a publishing company targeting children.

"In another instance, I was hired by management to help a woman in her midsixties who worked at an Internet company make the transition from working behind the desk to more public speaking on behalf of her company. The employee had white hair, and we added dimension to the color and gave her a new cut, freshening her look.

"Much of the time, what I've discovered is that people don't realize that we are all constantly in need of changing. We all need to keep making adjustments and advancements in the way we look through our twenties, thirties, forties, and fifties. What works at one age will be different at another. People focus on hair because it's lots easier to deal with than fashion or style."

Solomon thought it was obvious when people were "over-blonding." She said, "It looks like they are covering up some-thing. But you can't change one thing and not the others." As I listened, I realized that I had fallen into the very same trap. I'd let myself go gray, but I hadn't changed my clothing style or color palette. My discussion with Solomon convinced me that I was going to have to reassess the way I dressed.

When I finally asked whether she would have suggested, as my consultant, that I dye my hair, she said no. What she would have done is work with who and what I was and just make it bet-ter. "A sassier cut, the perfect crisp white shirt, and a steel gray or charcoal leather jacket." But not a *gold* leather jacket.

TWO IMAGE CONSULTANTS with very different personal styles and backgrounds had told me that my gray hair was okay. I was eager to see if the same would hold true at my downtown ap-pointment with StyleWorks of Union Square. The preappoint-ment questionnaire focused almost entirely on the nuts and bolts of my personal style, with only one set of personality questions asking me to select salient words such as "energetic," "business-like," "daring," "independent," or "glamorous" to describe my self-conception. I chose "energetic," "enthusiastic," "optimistic," "dependable," and "loyal," even though in the aggregate it made me sound like a good dog.

I met Carol Davidson, the owner of StyleWorks, in her 1970s residential high-rise (so apparently they mostly *do* work out of their apartments). She was in her midthirties and wore black leather pants (again, the leather), black flat boots, and a white blouse with turquoise jewelry. Leather pants and turquoise jewelry aside, we were on a similar wavelength. For this appointment, I costumed myself even more on the down-low, wearing my actual daily work-at-home uniform — baggy blue jeans, an old brown ribbed turtleneck sweater, the Merrells. I couldn't have looked less like a candidate for high-level corporate reentry if I had tried.

The initial consultation, at what now seemed a reasonable $375 for a two-hour session, began with a personalized presentation tabulating and analyzing the results of my questionnaire. I felt reassured that Davidson had taken the time to review my (purported) issues and objectives. She went into detail about the messages of colors: how we respond to value, intensity, and hue, as well as particular colors. Before talking with her, I would have assumed that I would intuitively know everything she would say about color — I was an art history major in college, so I had spent years studying the play of light and color in paintings, and what complementary colors did to and for each other. I considered, somewhat snobbishly, that I had a trained and pretty sophisticated eye. But, in fact, Carol related color to fabric weight and texture in a way that was wholly new to me, and valuable. She walked me through a primer on gauge of knit, fabric pattern, and garment lines and details. She had good visual aids that encapsulated various different styles of dressing: classic versus nonclassic, sporty versus feminine, traditional and elegant versus creative and dramatic.

She actually knew what she was talking about and organized the information lucidly and helpfully. It all made sense. Again I began to feel guilty that I had engaged Carol under false pretenses — and once again decided on the spot that I'd fess up. Even more, in fact, I'd come to realize through my previous two experiences that I *really did* want her to help me engineer a personal fashion makeover. I hadn't bought any new clothing in the ten years since I'd left my corporate job. Talk about a rut.

I told Carol that I was conducting research for a book about the ways in which women choose to age and was not really trying to reestablish myself as a corporate executrix. I confessed that I had half *wanted* her to tell me that I needed to dye my hair if I wished to get a big-time business job, or that I should "freshen" my look with some artificial color.

She paused. And finally said, "Oh, I would have been very disappointed if you'd indicated that you thought you should color your hair. It's very distinctive, and a strong statement."

Among the image consultants, I was now three for three on not dyeing my hair.

Until I talked with Lauren Solomon and Carol Davidson, I realized, I hadn't quite admitted to myself how insecure I was about how to make the best of the new, truer gray-haired version of myself. And although I was no longer engaging in the white lie of hair color, it didn't mean that I couldn't or shouldn't pay attention to the compensatory virtues of packaging in clothes, where the issue wasn't so much honesty as enhancing, or perhaps even creating, my personal style. Having gray hair didn't mean I couldn't also be stylish. It was time to fully flip the equation I had been living by. I'd believed that hair color and cut compensated for my rather shapeless and dowdy clothes. I now understood that hair dye didn't mask my extra weight or shabby attire. And Lauren was right—you can't change one thing and not adjust everything else. It was time to work with the complete me—using all of the tools (clothes, shoes, color, makeup, hairstyle) available to present an overall fresh and vibrant look.

Carol sat me in front of a sunny window and pulled out fabric patches to determine which colors made me look best, and it was amazing to me how modest, subtle shifts could make me appear very different. One shade of yellowish-green that I wore regularly made me look bruised and gaunt while a slightly different green with a blue tint made me look bright-eyed and healthy. I was chagrined that I hadn't figured out these differences on my own, but there's a reason we hire interior designers to help with our houses, and accountants to do our taxes.

I came to understand, sitting there in Davidson's office in Union Square, that the clothing and colors that had worked when I had artificially brown (and blond and red and black) hair and a corporate office in midtown really didn't reflect my life or coloring today. When I dyed my hair chestnut brown, I wore lots of chocolates and browns and rusts and reds and greens. I still owned those clothes but pretty much never wore them. After listening to Carol, I realized why—on some intuitive level, I knew that I didn't look good in them anymore. And it wasn't simply that they were out of style. The rich, somber clothing colors that had suited my old dark hair color didn't reflect my new sense of lightness. My actual coloring was now monochromatically soft and pale. I no longer had the sharp contrast in color between my fair skin and my dark hair that required the balance of deep color in my clothes. In that sunny room on 14th Street, I understood that it was time to chuck my old autumn palette of ambers and browns and rusts and mosses, and make room for new, soft blues and grays. Colors that would flatter the way I now looked with gray hair.

Carol uses the seasonal metaphors of the cosmetologist Bernice Kentner's *Color Me a Season* system to find the best tone and hue for clients' particular complexions and coloring and hair. Interestingly, in spite of my sense that I might now be more wintry in my look, it turns out I'm a summer. "The summer person," Kentner's book says, "has a very pale skin tone. Their paleness is often of great concern to them because they look tired and washed out in the wrong colors.... Summer's skin usually has a transparent look to it. They have a delicate look in soft pastel colors. When wearing dark, unbecoming colors, dark circles appear under the eyes and all the imperfections of the skin stand out....Color does more for a summer person than any other Season."

Which is precisely what I had seen so starkly that afternoon in Davidson's office. So blues, purples, and muted reds were good shades for me from now on—no more browns, rusts, or yellow-based greens. I wouldn't wear much pattern because my hair now had a lot of natural "pattern" to it. I left StyleWorks with a specific action plan detailing the six essential pieces of new clothing (two pairs of three-season pants, one black, one navy; one good navy dress; two pairs of better-fitting jeans; and a navy silk shirt) that I'd need to add to my wardrobe to jibe with and enhance my new hair color and serve as the foundation for a classic, crisp, age-appropriate everyday wardrobe.

All of the image consultants also offered a home service, to come and help winnow out your wardrobe so that you are left only with clothing that makes you look your best. I felt comfortable enough with Davidson after my initial consultation to invite her to do this with me. This is something I should have tackled years ago but always put off, preferring to shift the same, perpetually unworn 75 percent of my summer and winter clothes, season after season, back and forth from one closet to another, a foolishly space- and time-wasting semiannual ritual, especially in a compact New York house with limited closets.

As I was pruning back clearly out-of-date or unwearable clothes before Davidson arrived (I didn't want to use any more of her post–initial consultation $150-an-hour fee than necessary), it dawned on me that the process I'd gone through with my hair was analogous to the one I was now going through with my clothes. Both experiences were about looking squarely at myself and honestly cataloging what I saw: a fifty-year-old woman who should have gray hair, who lived a relaxed life, and whose priorities were, in order, family, friends, and work.

I'd been unable to part with my big-shoulder-padded, front-pleated Giorgio Armani or Calvin Klein suits from the '90s because I hadn't been prepared to acknowledge how completely my life had changed. Those expensive suits, so hard-earned, had been my reward for making it up the corporate ladder. They were powerful symbols of personal accomplishment and of my ability to take care of myself as effectively as any man. They vibrated in my closet, calling out to me that I could always go back. That I once had been something.

Not long after I had quit my corporate job, I was sitting on the subway at midday, in jeans and beat-up old loafers, thinking, as I looked at all of the other ragtag, clearly not "professional" people on the train with me, that I had fallen off the grid. It was a dark thought in a subterranean and dark, transitory place. No one had any idea who I was or where I was. It was a spring day, and when I came aboveground in Greenwich Village, the street was alive with people and sunshine, and I had a revelation that there were millions of people living very happy, nontraditional, non-nine-to-five lives. That moment was the beginning for me of finding my way in a freelance world of possibilities rather than certainties. My notion of success shifted from acknowledgment of external accomplishments to recognition of internal ones.

Sorting through my clothes before Carol's arrival was another such moment.

As I pulled each of those suits out of the closet, I realized they'd lost their emotional power over me. Not only did they no longer tempt me with their taint of busy meetings and lunches but they now actively repelled me. They felt stale and old and *heavy.* I didn't have a job to wear anymore.

Yet when Davidson came over, I still dutifully tried on a lot of those suits to see if any of them could be tailored to feel contemporary (they were too expensive to let go of without feeling I'd at least tried to use them), but I quickly realized it simply wouldn't be possible. I had just changed too much—physically and mentally.

At the same time, I pulled out a lot of the designer clothing that I inherited from my mother and grandmother. For sentimental reasons, I had kept a lot of their finer things—Chanel suits and Yves Saint Laurent blouses. With the clarity of the moment, I also saw that those particular kinds of luxe clothes, my designated Kansas City–style legacy, weren't the new me either. Luckily, my younger daughter, Lucy, who has her own natural, vintage-shop-meets-H&M-meets-Anthropologie style, loved a lot of my mother's clothes and kept them. When I see her looking hip rather than dowdy wearing my mother's 1966 Chanel sweaterdress over her jeans, I am thrilled—but not as much as I am that I've rid myself of some ghosts of my past.

There is no question that I would never have had the courage to face up to the ways in which my life had changed had I not been forced into the intense level of introspection that my year of letting my hair go gray imposed on me. By the time Davidson left my house that afternoon, I had hardly a thing left that I could wear, but I did look good in and *love* every item that remained. And just as I'd felt light and nimble when I finally cut off my last inches of colored hair, I now felt unaccountably joyful having purged the unnecessary emotionally laden fashion baggage. The sense of liberation was profound.

The Slippery Slope

So I rediscovered my inner clotheshorse. I started splurging on Crème de la Mer lotion — after all, I'm saving a ton of money by not coloring my hair. I do wear some minimal makeup. I want to look good — a healthy and pretty fifty-one. Deciding how I ought to look, finding that comfortable line for myself between indulging my vanity and maintaining my authenticity, is not a matter of embracing some all-or-nothing black-and-white doctrine.

We don't have to decide between being unshaven, unstyled, and all natural or being dyed, Brazilian-waxed, botoxed, restylaned, and surgically enhanced. We each have to find our own comfortable place. But the made-over, youth-craving side of the equation is definitely a slippery slope, where a modest submission to repackaging can seem to justify the next, more radical step, and then that one, the next, and on and on.

"I think," my husband said one day not long ago, very husbandishly, "that it's like the difference between rebuilding versus upkeep and maintenance. Shaving legs or depilating or wearing makeup is maintenance, like repointing the bricks. And I guess you could argue that hair color is in that latter category, too — but to me, it's different, because the color of one's hair is such a profoundly noticeable, ever-present, and primary expression of who one is. The idea underlying artificial hair color is that gray on a woman — but not a man, mostly, not yet — is a flaw, a blemish, an embarrassment to be hidden, a problem to be fixed. To me, coloring gray hair is like painting over the brick or stone or cedar shingles on a nice old house — it's not necessarily awful, but part of the beautiful essence of the real thing is how it looks as it ages. It's why we love old cities like Paris and Rome."

But the line isn't clear. One woman's gut rehab is another's prettifying upkeep. If the path back from cosmetic illusion is filled with unanticipated consequences, so, too, is the road forward. If I color my hair, shouldn't I fix my frown lines? If Linda has a brow lift, should I? And if I zap my varicose veins, then why not do a tummy tuck? No examination of aging and authenticity in the early twenty-first century can avoid the elephant in the room — plastic surgery. Trust me, I'm embarrassed to say, I know from personal experience.

When I turned forty, around the time I dyed my hair shoe-polish black, my then five-year-old daughter needed to have plastic surgery to repair the facial scarring from a hemangioma birthmark she'd had as an infant. So there we were, in the plush, seductive privacy of an Upper East Side surgeon's office. As long as I was already there, and very much feeling forty—God, *forty*—I thought I'd ask the surgeon about the little Deputy Dawg pooches that had started to form at the corners of my mouth. Hmm, guess what? Without missing a beat or waving off my moment of anxious vanity, he said he could "take care of it."

The surgeon and I certainly didn't have the "What do you expect to get out of this surgery?" conversation that opens each episode of the TV series *Nip/Tuck.* If we had, I imagine I would have voiced a vague sentiment such as "I just want to look better." But this surgeon simply said he'd "fix" me, and I never gave a moment's thought to the source or sense of my anxiety over the inevitable, tiny sags.

Instead, for the now-that-I-have-college-tuition-to-pay insane price of $5,000, I underwent the surgery. And by "surgery," I don't mean that I saw a scalpel or sutures but rather that the saggy mouth fat was "sucked" out in a miniliposuction performed in his office. And then, at the doctor's suggestion, "as long as we were doing that work," I had a bit of fat siphoned from my right hip and injected into my nasal-labial folds—that is, the grooves that run from the nostrils to the lip. My chin and neck were bruised a lovely shade of chartreuse. Within two weeks, the bruises were gone and the clumpy injected fat had settled—and neither my family nor I could see a whit of difference from before my surgery.

From no one did I get even one comment such as "My, you look well-rested." Of course, it never occurred to me at the time that my black, evil-twin hair color washed my skin tone out so that I looked chronically exhausted no matter what I did. Later, friends who were more experienced with plastic surgery told me that the best way to maximize the surgery's visible impact was to change hairstyles at the same time. That way people noticed the new hair without attributing the new, improved you to the surgery. The need to resort to such sleight of hand to obscure the plastic surgery while simultaneously drawing attention to it is a funny, twisted, very modern-day stratagem.

After the procedure, I *immediately* felt embarrassed by my degree of vanity. In a scene that would be plausible in a Woody Allen film, as I was leaving, I spotted a friend—or thought I did—on the street outside the doctor's office, so I lurked in the foyer until I was certain that she couldn't see me dash out to get a taxi. My mortification that people I knew might discover what I had done was message enough to me that I'd crossed my line in terms of what I was comfortable doing to look younger. Until now, apart from my family, I've told only one good friend about that episode. In retrospect, it was a classic midlife-crisis moment.

And although I have never had any other plastic surgery, I did have three $700 Botox treatments over the course of my forty-seventh, forty-eighth, and forty-ninth years. My family, the only people I told I was getting the treatments, insisted that the shots made no difference in the way I looked. And in the end, I decided they actually made me look slightly worse, a little weird, off-kilter, *shiny*. My brow looked more prominent in a not-wholly-attractive Klingonesque way, and when I made any dramatic facial gesture, my *upper* forehead seemed to be *unusually* wrinkled. The creases didn't go away; they just moved north. I resisted that literal slippery slope, the temptation to chase after the remaining creases and inject still more Botox so that I'd be perpetually, entirely *smooth*.

As with any large cultural change, the old stigmas and taboos recede and the new values arise incrementally, small peer group by small peer group. With regard to cosmetic fibs—first face powder; then hair color, dermabrasion, teeth veneers, and injections; and finally plastic surgery (and, one wonders, what's *next*)—tiny individual tipping points about what's acceptable and desirable happen among ten friends, then a hundred acquaintances, then whole demographic sectors. Before long, there is a new normal. In the national survey I conducted for this book, of four hundred women, average age forty-nine, 15 percent reported having had cosmetic injections or surgery—probably about the same percentage of middle-aged women who, back in the '50s when the artificial-coloring boom began, dyed their hair.

My husband and I had free tickets to a big weeklong conference in Aspen last July, at which all sorts of movers and shakers from government, business, nonprofits, the academy, and media lectured and appeared on panels. The paying attendees were nearly all rich people over forty-five, very well-groomed men and women who flew in from LA and elsewhere to vacation or spend the whole summer in Aspen. As we waited one afternoon for the audience to gather for a talk by Bill Clinton, my husband found himself studying the faces of the women, a good half of which had been noticeably reshaped by surgeons. And he noticed a phenomenon that had never occurred to either of us before: because we now *expect* upper-class female sixty-five- and seventy-five-year-olds to have the perpetually surprised-looking facial expression of cosmetic surgery—that's just how (rich) older women *look* these days—forty-five- and fifty-five-year-old women who have the same, pseudogirlish, artificially wide-eyed facial tautness now read as *old.* Such a perverse unintended consequence!

"If you spend enough time looking at the women on TV news and interview shows," said my friend Bruce Feirstein, the screenwriter, "you realize that unnatural has become the new natural. Not just perfect teeth—preternaturally tight skin and eyebrows that don't do much moving. So nobody thinks much about this anymore, unless we're talking about triple-D cups or obvious cases of surgeons-gone-wild."

After all, the late Peter Jennings, one of broadcast journalism's embodiments of gravitas, famously had his eyes tweaked by a cosmetic surgeon. "A forty-year-old in Dallas," Bruce said, "looks at a forty-year-old on TV, be it in news or entertainment, who looks thirty, and it's a whole new round of body-image questions. Nobody on TV ages; why should you?"

Back in the day, TV's messages about elective plastic surgery tended to be more negative. When I was in grade school, I saw two episodes of *The Twilight Zone* that made me think about beauty in ways I hadn't considered. "The Eye of the Beholder" opens in a 1960 hospital room with a young woman's face completely covered in gauze after a plastic-surgical procedure. The young woman says from under the gauze, "I never really wanted to be beautiful. I just wanted people not to scream when they looked at me." Her doctor muses to the nurse, "What is the dimensional difference between beauty and something repellent? Why shouldn't people be allowed to be different?" The attending nurses and physicians hover around the patient, worrying that the operation will have failed and that she will emerge as ugly as she was before and unsalvageable. We see only the backs of the nurses and doctors. The audience is left to imagine what the woman's horrible disfigurement might be. Eventually her bandages are removed, and we see the perfect face of a classically beautiful young Grace Kelly / Sandra Dee type. The nurses and doctors are audibly aghast and horrified. And only then, as they turn their heads, do we see that they all have hideous pig faces. The "ugly" girl will be sent to live in a leper-colony-like reservation, where she and "others of her kind" can live out their days.

My other most-memorable *Twilight Zone* episode, "Number Twelve Looks Just Like You," is set in a future in which everyone, at age nineteen, is surgically renovated by plastic surgeons to conform to one of a few ideal physical types. "What young girl," Rod Serling says in his introduction, "wouldn't happily exchange a plain face for a lovely one? What girl could refuse the opportunity to be beautiful? For want of a better estimate, let's call it the year 2000. At any rate, imagine a world where modern science has developed a means of giving everyone the face and body he dreams of." The protagonist, again a young woman, wants to keep the face with which she was born—a desire considered pathologically neurotic in this conformist, prettiness-worshipping, strenuously happy twenty-first-century society. Her father had chosen suicide over accepting one of the new, certified-handsome faces, but she finds she lacks the will to bear up against the social pressure and picks Number Eight, the same as her best friend. Rod Serling, as always, returns at the end with his narrator's coda: "Portrait of a young lady in love with herself. Improbably? Perhaps. But in an age of plastic surgery and bodybuilding and an infinity of cosmetics, let us hesitate to say impossible. These and other strange blessings may be waiting for us in the future—which, after all, is *The Twilight Zone*." This episode first aired in 1964, when I was eight.

I don't think I'm wrong to see those shows as uncomfortably visionary. We're not there *quite yet,* but during the last four decades, the real world has definitely moved toward *The Twilight Zone.* Extrapolate the trend line, double the available technologies, and imagine the choices and pressures our great-grandchildren may face...

WENDY LEWIS IS THE AUTHOR of eight books on beauty, and she's probably the best-known cosmetic-surgery consultant. She calls herself the "knife coach." She charges people, the majority of which are women, $250 for an hour-long telephone interview and up to $1,000 for a more comprehensive package, advising them about what particular cosmetic surgeries and injections they ought to seek out and in what sequence, how much they should spend for the various interventions, and how to pick doctors. And Lewis is a highly extended brand—in addition to her books and one-on-one consultations, she offers a $9.95 annual subscription to a quarterly *Nip & Talk* newsletter, giving up-to-the-minute information about the state of the art, and also provides a reader-question feature on her Web site called "Ask the Beauty Junkie."

At the time we met, Wendy was forty-seven and a proud walking advertisement for her profession. She was open about her tummy tucks and regular use of Botox, Restylane, and collagen. She somewhat sheepishly confessed to me that her fourteen-year-old daughter didn't want her friends to come over to the house after her mother had had her lips done. "It was too scary."

I was up front with Lewis and told her the truth about my book and the research I was conducting into all the issues surrounding gray hair. "If you were my client," she said the moment we'd sat down for coffee, "the first thing I'd tell you to do is color your hair." *But...she's a* surgery *consultant!* "It really ages you. Your skin isn't too bad, but your hair is aging." Her candor, as she saw it, was "empowering" me. "But I guess one woman's 'empowerment,'" she added, "is another's elective slavery."

Lewis sees herself as a truth teller. She is not a therapist, she said, and she doesn't cross that line, but she did say that, not surprisingly, her consultations "are very intimate. People really let their hair down." On the one hand, she has no patience for the client who comes in wanting "to look like Meg Ryan"—an odd choice of celebrity example, I thought, given Ryan's much-discussed cosmetic procedures. "You have to work with what you've got and be realistic."

But she also sees a dangerous trend in which surgeons don't really turn people down anymore. "If a client asks them to do something, they say, 'Yeah, I could do that,'" just as my top-of-the-line surgeon had done a decade ago with my teensy procedure. "They tend not to think, *Is this surgery right for this woman?* because they know the woman can go next door and get the same surgery from someone else." Lewis wants her clients to understand the profit motive in the transaction. "I think the business has become commoditized, with laser clinics in strip malls. The treatments are completely mainstream, the beauty business has become franchised, and they are now in the business of monetizing their expensive lasers."

Yet, of course, Lewis herself profits from the new plethora of offerings and the resulting market boom—helping people decide from among the proliferating laser treatments, skin fillers, and surgical procedures. Women often can't articulate what they want or why, "so I try to help them figure out what the mission is. People want to look like their younger selves—they feel they lose credibility if they don't. But I also want them to be realistic about what it will take and what it will mean. It's completely unrealistic for mothers of the bride to come to me three months before the wedding and say that they want to look their best on the day and need a face-lift, tummy tuck, and breast enhancement.

I tell them they've got time for only one thing, and photographs will be the most important things, so do the lift."

She says she sees clients from most economic strata but says that the richer they are, the more vulnerable they are to the influences of their peers. "It is not a pure correlation, but it is harder to resist having work done if you begin to feel you look older than your peers who have had work done." And "if your husband sees every woman around him in your set with a smooth brow and full lips, then he'll begin to wonder why you don't have them. Once everyone has had something done, then no one thinks it is unusual."

Lewis thinks that the "women who get hit the hardest as they age are the most attractive women — they've relied on their looks to give them a competitive edge with both women and men, and at fifty, depression sets in. They didn't anticipate their beauty going away."

I asked Lewis the median age of her clients. "In '97," she said, "when I started my business, the average age was fifty. Now it's down a decade — even people in their thirties want maintenance, and eighteen-year-olds want boob jobs. The core customer has expanded on both ends — demographically there is no cutoff anymore unless someone older is not in good health. The number of people in the space is large." *Hello, Rod Serling.*

SUSANNA MOORE HELPED me get a fix on the slippery slope of cosmetic procedures. As I mentioned, Susanna worked part-time as a model and actress in the 1960s, and today, at sixty-one, remains beautiful. One afternoon over tea, I asked what choices she had made along the way. "I had my eyes done at forty-eight after I saw a photo of myself and my eyebrow was just hanging over my eye." Susanna also had silicone shots between her brows and around her eyes and mouth at least six times a year during her thirties. She credits her relatively unlined forehead of today to that regime. Botox never tempted her because the thought of putting that poison into her system scared her. She was utterly aware of the irony of saying that she wouldn't do an FDA-approved treatment but would "do the silicone treatment today if it were legal. I once did Restalyne in my lips, and it was grotesque. I looked like an ape. In fact," she added, "I've become sort of anti–plastic surgery, and I'm too old. You have to do it early, and I'm glad I did my eyes when I did because today I think it would show." I asked if her female friends have had plastic surgery. "Yes, every single one, and several have gone multiple times—and that is very painful to watch." She sipped her tea. "I find that my vanity has become predicated or voiced by *not* doing any of the treatments. Now I'm vain about *not* doing it."

It's a Guy Thing, Too

FOR THE MOMENT, men have it easier when it comes to the decision whether to dye or not to dye. Anderson Cooper, the forty-year-old CNN anchor, famously wrote about and traded on the topic of having gray hair as a youngish, attractive man.

"I don't get it, but gray on guys drives a lot of folks wild," he wrote in *Details*.

> The other thing that happens when you start getting gray: You begin checking out every other gray-haired guy....
>
> This can deteriorate into something of an obsession. For a while, every time I saw Phil Donahue, I had to reassure myself: It's okay. I'm not as gray as he is....
>
> You can, of course, dye. Plenty of guys do, but if you ask me, you might as well advertise your desperation.

Why not just wear a button that says "I sit in a salon once a month with silver foil in my hair"?

You can also try dyeing your hair at home, but isn't there something sad about habitually locking yourself in the bathroom and doling out dye into your trembling hands like some aging junkie?

My advice? Give in to gray.

He was speaking to men, of course — *Details*-reading men, but still. For men, "Give in to gray" remains unremarkable counsel, common sense, and a fairly easy choice. For men, the old normal is still mainly normal. Our double standard concerning gray hair is, at this point, far more extreme than that concerning sexual behavior or work outside the home.

In fact, Anderson Cooper's gray hair has been an advantage for him, lending him the image of seriousness that Anna Quindlen talked about and, because it was so unusual to see someone his age with gray hair, a striking, positive market differentiation — if he's so "real" about his looks, he must be telling the truth about the news. There is no question he would have less anchorman authority if he dyed his hair.

And it works for older men as well. The longtime, standard-issue local LA anchorman Steve Edwards had consistently and plainly fake brown hair for years — but recently, past sixty, he stopped coloring, and it's now entirely gray-white. He looks vastly better — not just "distinguished" but more real, believable.

A big deal was made about the prematurely gray-haired thirty-year-old Taylor Hicks winning *American Idol*. During Hicks's initial audition, Simon Cowell told him he would never make it to the final round—because, Cowell said, he just didn't look the part of a young pop singer. But in the event, Hicks's hair perfectly complemented his Joe Cocker–esque geekiness, and the voting audience found that total package—awkward mannerisms, slight paunch, gravelly Alabama voice, *and* gray hair—refreshingly authentic. The gray, which visually differentiated him from everyone else who had ever appeared on *American Idol,* gave him a competitive edge.

Who thinks George Clooney, Jon Stewart, Green Bay quarterback Brett Favre, Richard Gere, Mark Harmon, Kris Kristofferson, Paul Newman, or Steve Martin isn't sexy? No woman on earth would say to herself, *I'd date Clooney except for that gray hair—he just looks too old.*

Which is not to say that men don't care about their hair. In my survey, the male respondents spent, on average, about $1,000 a year on hair care, and a full quarter of them said they didn't like their hair (versus 20 percent of women). But it's complicated for guys. *GQ* ran a 2005 feature entitled "Gray Is the New Black"—but also had men writing in to the style adviser, asking whether they should dye their gray chest hair. So what's a guy to do?

For all of the double standards associated with aging—gray hair on men is *distinguished;* a little paunch can be *sexy*—I think it's going to become more and more challenging for men to resist the marketing tsunami coming their way. According to a Mind-Branch market research report, the home-hair-care market is worth $1.54 billion, and since the women's market is saturated, men's hair-coloring products are now the fastest-growing segment.

Grecian Formula, introduced in 1961, about the same time as the women's at-home hair-coloring market was ramping up, is the punch-liney legacy brand, but today the market is filled with products—Clairol's Men's Choice and Natural Instincts color lines, Redken's for Men's Color Camo, L'Oréal's ColorSpa for Men, Garnier Nutrisse, Herbal Essences, Pinaud-Clubman, GreyBan Anti-Grey Solution. The market leader, Just for Men, has recently partnered with *Maxim*—the humorous, aggressively anti-BS, T and A men's magazine with a median-age readership of just *twenty-seven*—to introduce hair dye targeting the young demo.

And the other night, as I was making dinner and watching *NBC Nightly News,* the following message stopped me mid-potato-peel: "Just for Men stops your hair from hiding who you are."

What?

I was used to mentally blocking out the osteoporosis, erectile-dysfunction, and menopause ads that clutter the evening news (which are reminders that people fifty and over are perhaps the only ones who *watch* the news). But I couldn't believe that an advertiser was now directly telling *men* that simply by having gray hair, they weren't *themselves.* During *60 Minutes* the same week, I heard a different variation of the Just for Men ad: "When it's a big event, does she see gray or the real you?" "Stay in the game." *Hello? Do women not see Patrick Dempsey as "in the game"?*

There's a prevalent notion in our culture that men cannot possibly find women with gray hair attractive, and now, with this campaign, Just for Men is using that negative image to manipulate men into believing that it is true for them as well — and doing so by insisting that the fib of artificial color is actually a means to a deeper truth.

About seventy million American men are older than thirty-five, and according to industry research, thirteen million of them color their hair — almost one in five. Even in Raleigh, North Carolina, a quintessentially middle-American city, the owner of the hair salon Blo says that 35 percent of his male clientele now color their hair.

Sertac Ozrulay, the colorist at his father's fancy Washington, DC, salon, told me it was the rare man who *enjoyed* having his hair done at their salon. "It's just too public. Chris Matthews" — the sixty-one-year-old blond and one of the Ozrulays' clients — "is one of the few who doesn't seem to have a problem with people seeing him here." Ozrulay says that among his clientele, most men color their hair for about five years, and then they just quit — the maintenance is too challenging. Some of his clients demand that he leave what he calls the "Paulie from *The Sopranos*" white wings at their temples in order to make them better pass for natural. *Hello? Can they be serious?* "I have to say, though, that it's a great thing financially for me to have men coloring their hair."

And men who dye their hair tend to do it more often than women, both because they have more frequent haircuts and because they wish to avoid the emergence of any gray roots, thereby achieving a more convincingly real color. Unlike women, for whom color is permitted to exist along a broad spectrum between authentic-looking and obviously unreal, nearly all men color their hair as pure fakery—only their hairdressers (and maybe their wives) know for sure. In this realm, men are where women were a generation ago. Guys sitting around at a bar or the office cafeteria just aren't going to be talking about their fabulous new hair color.

Not unless they're men like, say, the fashion designer Isaac Mizrahi. When I talked with him, he described how he started coloring about two years before, at age forty-three, after someone had suggested that he make his natural dark-brown color richer. He told me that the "next thing I want to do is bleach my hair a gorgeous walnut color. Marcello Mastroianni had it in *The 10th Victim,* and I've wanted it ever since I saw the movie." Mizrahi believes that men are dyeing their hair now "because they *can.* We've come to a point where men take care of the kids, and they can cry, so they can also color their hair."

One day I was visiting my friend Jeff, the ravingly heterosexual television writer who also occasionally appears on TV, and I found a discarded Just for Men box in his bathroom wastebasket. He is, I discovered, unabashed about doing it and loves to discuss all the nuances of color with me.

Strange, isn't it? As women became more legally and socially "equal" to men during the second half of the last century, coloring their gray hair became more and more obligatory. And now a strange equality is creeping in from the other direction, as more and more men feel obliged to tell the same white lie as women, coloring their hair.

It's disconcerting to me that men are feeling this pressure and will be urged on ever more by the marketers. My father and my father-in-law both had great heads of white hair (as well as extremely self-confident bearings), and when either one of them entered a room, people often turned and studied them, as if they were well known — *Senator or Governor Somebody,* I always imagined strangers thinking. And conversely, artificial color on men tends to leave exactly the opposite impression. Today, with gray hair not yet being impermissible for men, those who color their hair and don't admit it — unlike the candid Jeff — seem more than a little desperate, like the mortifying portraits Anderson Cooper paints.

At a Manhattan dinner party one evening, I was seated next to a famous and vigorous writer, then seventy-seven, and as I was telling him about this book, he asked me, in all seriousness, "Do you think *men* are doing this?" I tried not to glance at his unnaturally pink-hued hair and simply said, "Well, yes — I think you'd be really surprised at who's doing it."

Figuring Out Where You Stand—The Fountain of Youth Index

REMEMBER HOW I ADMITTED, for twenty-odd years of coloring my hair, I studiously avoided calculating the expense? Remember that when I finally did the calculation, I was horrified to discover that I'd spent $65,000? It's not that during those years my income didn't vary wildly—it did. With the exception of my last few years at Nickelodeon in the early '90s, I did not make a lot of money. It was simply that having my hair look its best—and by "best," I mean "not gray"—was always nonnegotiable, off the table regardless of my income.

I was not alone. I discovered in my survey (which included people from ages twenty to eighty-two in California, Wyoming, Kansas, Missouri, Indiana, Ohio, Pennsylvania, New Jersey, New York, Connecticut, Massachusetts, Maryland, Georgia, and Florida) that women who earned between $25,000 and $50,000 spent an average of $60 a month on their hair color alone—yet women in the $100,000 to $250,000 bracket spent only marginally more, $70 a month on average. That is, women in the middle and lower economic strata spent nearly as much as the extremely well-to-do—nearly 3 percent of their incomes went toward coloring their hair. This is a stark example of what economists call "inelasticity"—a spending dynamic ordinarily limited to essential goods such as groceries and medicine and gasoline.

We asked the survey respondents, if money becomes tight in your household, which luxuries are you willing to do without in order to keep dyeing your hair? Of those who answered the question, the large majority said they'd be at least a little willing to forgo things such as eating out at restaurants, going to movies, and buying new clothes or a new car *before* they'd give up dyeing their hair.

My investment in *time* in getting my hair dyed was also huge—three or four hours a month, or a thousand hours in all over twenty years. (About the same amount of time as I've spent on this book, which at least has a nice symmetry.) I discovered that the average woman in my survey spends even more time, 7.9 hours a month, coloring her hair—versus 7.8 hours a month having sex.

In the survey, I asked each woman to tote up how much time and money she spent monthly on the following: exercise classes, gyms, personal training, exercise/sports equipment, exercise clothing, massage/bodywork, makeup, waxing, antiaging products, cellulite creams, facials, dermatologic procedures (microdermabrasion, Botox, fillers, laser treatments, etc.), skin creams, shampoos, conditioners, salon styling—and, of course, dyeing in salons and at home.

I tallied the responses, clustering them according to the total amount of money and time the survey respondents spent making themselves look and feel physically better. This resulted in four basic lifestyle groups—what I call the Skeptics, the Doers, the Followers, and the Preservers.*

The Skeptics spend the least amount of time *and* money on their personal appearance. They are the most doubtful about or indifferent to the promises made by marketers for products that promote being buff, burnished, and young-looking. They want to look good but with the least amount of fuss and effort. If they were a car, they'd be a Saturn or a Prius. A third of Skeptics are divorced or widowed. They are lawyers, researchers, or educators; have the lowest average incomes; worry most about caring for their parents as they age; and devote the least amount of time to exercising (an average of twenty-five hours per month), to hair coloring (three hours per month), and to hair styling (fewer than five hours per month), yet they still spend substantially on hair color, an average of $37 a month. Skeptics tend to choose to be brunettes. The older women they admire are classic icons, such as Joanne Woodward and Diane Keaton, and they are the one group who listed their husbands as gray-haired men they admire. They also think it's wrong that some professions demand a youthful

*Go to www.AnneKreamer.com/book_surveyintro.html to find out what you are.

appearance. Skeptics can be a bit sanctimonious about their "purity" and tend in general to be reverse snobs.

The Doers, named because they devote lots of time to exercise and fitness activities, are focused on the health benefits more than the beauty benefits of exercise. If they were a car, they'd be a Saab or an Audi—high performance, sleek design, European style. They're a bit older than the average respondent, with an average age of fifty-three, and they are more likely to be married. They have job titles such as artist, chef, and massage therapist. Their average income is second lowest of the four clusters—but unlike the relatively sedentary Skeptics, they average *sixty two* hours a month exercising. Doers spend time more than money on looking youthful. They are early adopters of new fitness regimens—they do Pilates, yoga, weight training, and cardio workouts every week. The older women they admire are, not surprisingly, the aggressively fit and entrepreneurial Madonna and the aggressively authentic Jamie Lee Curtis. Like Skeptics, Doers think it's unfortunate that some professions demand a youthful appearance. Fitness can be a narcotic for Doers, and if not careful they can become pedantic evangelists in their views about health.

The Followers are the youngest of the four groups—average age: forty-three—and have the financial means but apparently not the time or patience or willpower to invest the hours Doers spend on athletic activities. I call this group the Followers because they seem most influenced by media imagery and information. Most Followers describe themselves as homemakers. Their average household income is the highest, and 90 percent of them live in suburbs. Followers read magazines voraciously. They keep up with and embrace most forever-young techniques—in many instances drawing the line only at extreme measures such as full face-lifts. If they were a car, they might be a Lexus. They spend the least amount of time exercising—nineteen hours a month. They spend the least on salon hair color as well, $28 a month—in large part, it seems, because they are almost a decade younger and less naturally gray than the others. But when they dye, unlike the Skeptics or the Doers, the color of choice is blond. The older people they admire are Diane Sawyer and Sean Connery. And they don't mind that some professions require a youthful look.

The Preservers are the oldest group, with an average age of nearly fifty-four. And the majority are married. They work as interior designers, marketers, and publishing executives. Their incomes are the second highest, and half live in cities. If Preservers were a car, they'd be a Jaguar or Porsche—impressive-looking and high maintenance. They spend the second-most time exercising (twenty-six hours a month), and they spend more than anyone else on hair color, almost $90 per month—with a decided color preference, like the Followers, for blond. Preservers, so called because they go to the greatest lengths to maintain a youthful appearance, do more than just read about the newest antiaging techniques—they schedule face-lifts and tummy tucks during their vacations. They run the risk of becoming cosmetic-surgery fanatics. The older women they admire are Jaclyn Smith and Lauren Hutton. Like Followers, they think it's fine that some professions require a youthful look. Alone among the four groups, Preservers specifically mention "going gray" as a primary fear connected to aging.

In parentheses in the graphic below are the percentages of the total sample that each group constitutes. Combined, those percentages add up to only 68 percent because the other 32 percent of respondents did not fall clearly into a single group but instead embodied "mixtures" of characteristics from more than one group.

There are, of course, blurry boundaries and flux between adjacent groups. For instance, I took my own poll twice, once as I

<table>
<tr><td colspan="2" rowspan="4" style="vertical-align:top">MONEY SPENT ↑</td></tr>
</table>

The Followers (15%)	The Preservers (9%)
The Skeptics (29%)	The Doers (15%)

MONEY SPENT

TIME SPENT →

began to go gray at forty-nine and again when I was almost fifty-one. The first time I answered, when I was still coloring my hair every three weeks, I came out a solid Follower, because I was spending so much money on purely aesthetic products and activities such as hair dye and salon visits and dermatologist treatments, and not much time on exercises such as yoga and walking. The second time I took the survey—after I'd stopped coloring my hair and started going to the gym several times a week, forty hours a month—I was a Doer. It was interesting that in my survey, an overwhelming 97 percent of the respondents answered that they would rather be thin and gray than overweight with colored hair. Essentially, I forced myself to make that hypothetical choice real.

French Women Do Go Gray

Thinking about all of the trade-offs that we American women make in the course of trying to maintain some semblance of youthfulness made me curious about whether the story was different in Europe, particularly France.

I am *so* American, and I *so* wish I were more French. After marinating my young-adult self in books such as Colette's *Chéri* and François Sagan's *Bonjour Tristesse,* and in the films of Catherine Deneuve, Isabel Adjani, and Juliette Binoche, a certain kind of French woman became my de facto benchmark against which all female sexiness was measured. French women, to me, were all about being inherently stylish and beautiful without great artifice, women who could make a man swoon with the barest arch of an eyebrow or flick of cigarette ash.

Karl is a thirty-eight-year-old American media executive who has spent the last fifteen years living in Greece, Norway, and Britain. When I asked him what European women did to maintain a youthful appearance, he joked, "Smoke cigarettes."

The success of Mireille Guiliano's *French Women Don't Get Fat,* with over a million hardcover books sold in the United States alone, clearly illustrates that I shared this longing with lots of my peers. Guiliano's message reinforced my image of the sophisticated and sensual French woman and also really resonated with the newly gray me. Her mantra to find pleasure in everything you do and to deeply savor the good (high-quality, fine dark chocolate versus crappy, merely high-caloric candy bars) and sensual things (the heady fragrance of fresh rosemary) felt intuitively correct. Her whole sense of less-is-more found a willing adept in me. And as a New Yorker, I already walked everywhere, which she recommends.

I thought if anyone would have a take on how French women choose to age differently from Americans, it would be she. While Guiliano was on a promotional tour for her second book, *French Women for All Seasons: A Year of Secrets, Recipes, and Pleasure,* she and I had the following e-mail exchange:

ANNE: Mireille, do French women color their hair?
MIREILLE: France is a country of hairdressers. The number of *salons de coiffure* is incredible. Virtually every block in a city has one or more, and every little village has one or two. In our small village of fifteen

hundred people in Provence, there are two. Near our home in the heart of Paris, there are at least twenty-five within a five-minute walk. Going to the hairdresser is routine. I'd like to say weekly, though not for everyone, but for plenty of people it is. And while prices are reasonable compared with the U.S. (the effect of competition, no doubt), there are all sorts of products and things — oils, creams, colors, cuts, and techniques — that are offered (and pretty much pushed). Obviously the coiffeurs make lots of suggestions and certainly promote hair coloring, which is highly profitable. So, putting together all that I've just said, French women routinely color their hair — perhaps starting in their twenties, for fashionable streaking or tinting, and certainly when gray appears, to eliminate it. Clearly coloring is done both to look more stylishly individualistic ("beautiful" is not the right word…to look "good," for sure, but to look "individualistic" might be a better word) and, as one ages, to "freeze time." There is a phrase and period in France that I write about in *French Women for All Seasons* called *"entre deux âges,"* literally "between two ages," or of ambiguous age. That's where mature French women work to reside.

I do know that well-preserved, stylish women in their fifties and sixties who go all gray stand out. Their hair becomes a fashion statement. And I know hairdressers play around with gray streaking so people and their hair don't look either artificially young or old but perhaps *entre deux âges.*

ANNE: Do you think French women dye their hair as often as Americans? And do they use similar colors or different ones?

MIREILLE: I know that statistically 54 percent of American women color their hair, but I don't exactly know what that means. In some neighborhoods, it is probably 90 percent. Among women in their twenties, probably a tiny percentage. Anyway, I don't know the French statistic but suspect it is higher than in America.

Hair colors do differ in France. For starters, you do see a lot more carrot reds and a bit more mahogany reds. In general, you don't see nearly as much blond. France is not a country of blue-eyed blondes, nor are blue-eyed blondes the seeming envy of woman and man. I remember being told that when the French version of the game show *Wheel of Fortune* appeared, it had a Vanna White knockoff and didn't do well until they traded her in for a brunette. Brown hair is the norm in France.

ANNE: Is there any sense from you that French men view women with gray hair as any less attractive or sexually desirable?

MIREILLE: Well, as far as I can tell, gray hair isn't much of a factor. French men are less seduced by youth than American men and would rather flirt with women of all ages. Mature French women "of a certain age" are certainly still held up as sexually desirable.

ANNE: Or is it a nonfactor or perhaps even an asset?

MIREILLE: There is a sense, I am told, and that I read about and see, to a limited extent, that French men prefer "seasoned" women to young ones. It's the idea of experience and knowing who they are and what they want and [that they] are *bien dans sa peau* (comfortable in their skins) that is seductive. It is said that it makes them more ready for and appreciative of pleasure without the complications of youth. So, gray hair may be an asset. I'll leave the rest to psychoanalysts.

ANNE: My husband makes an analogy between a fabulous-looking building in Paris—we know it's old, we can see it's been plastered and repaired for centuries, and it is precisely that patina that makes European buildings so much more beautiful than American ones—and he relates that to the beauty to be found in an older woman. Is this a French sensibility?

MIREILLE: It is not an outward patina that is attractive but a kind of inward one. As I write in *French Women for All Seasons,* a French woman is most defined by her ease in being herself and the attractiveness that comes from relishing her pleasures. French women achieve this state more intuitively than most, but not everyone is successful. The secret of the woman who continues to be *bien dans sa peau* is that she has come to terms with enjoying each phase of her life and adjusting to life's different seasons. Age doesn't matter for those women who acquire self-confidence and an air of serenity, who adjust well to time and age and who embody that je ne sais quoi of the mythical French woman. Those inner layers are worn on their skin and everywhere, and are what is attractive.

ANNE: If you were to sum it all up with one thought about the difference between French and American women and how they choose to age, what might it be? **MIREILLE:** Americans are too often obsessed with youth and looking forever young (sometimes making serious mistakes in not dressing their age), and French women are more comfortable in coming to terms with each phase of their lives and adjusting to each of life's seasons. Confidence and individuality are big parts of a woman's "style."

Guiliano's take on French and European women confirmed some of my assumptions about how we and they differ in our approaches to beauty and aging—and jibed with the data that Dove, the skin- and hair-care division of the global consumer products company Unilever, discovered in their 2004 Global Study on Women, Beauty, and Well-Being.

The study, undertaken by a team led by researchers from Harvard and the London School of Economics, found that when women were asked to describe themselves, 43 percent of French women and 37 percent of Italians said they were "natural," versus only 21 percent of Americans. When they were asked if society pressured women to enhance their physical attractiveness, the responses again lined up: 75 percent of the Americans, 57 percent of the Italians, and 62 percent of the French said yes. Asked what products they used to feel more physically attractive, 84 percent of the American women reported using hair products versus 66 percent of the French.

According to another recent survey of French women, and counter to Mireille Guiliano's sense, a majority of women in France still *don't* dye their hair. A well-to-do, fifty-five-year-old, American-educated French friend of mine, Claire, now living in London and a recent convert to her natural gray after years of dyeing, affirmed this when we spoke. She estimates that no more than a third of French women she knows color their hair. "I believe this fantasy about Frenchmen finding women of all ages sexy is true. It all has to do with style and elegance and maybe a flirtatious attitude."

And it does appear that, gray or colored hair aside, European culture does accept sexy older women more easily than ours does. It seems telling that Diane Keaton's *Something's Gotta Give* grossed $20 million more overseas than in America. I asked Jason, a thirty-year-old Englishman I know, if he thought younger European men found gray-haired women attractive. "It depends. Anne Bancroft in *The Graduate* was hot, and a lady I work with had some gray, and she was attractive as well. I do think Englishmen are more adventurous." Jason enthusiastically went on to share a story that sounded like a scene from a Hugh Grant movie. "I had some friends who used to go to a club in Essex called Dukes and see who was the oldest woman they could get home. Unfortunately it backfired when one went round to his friend's house the next morning to find his date from the previous evening answering the door. It was his friend's mother." *Awkward.*

Nick, Jason's dad and a former television colleague of mine, lives in London with his girlfriend and was a bit more thoughtful than his son about the differences between American and European attitudes toward aging. Like my husband, he thinks that the densely textured, old-fashioned fabric of European towns and cities themselves—the different architectures from different centuries—fosters a richer range of acceptable beauty than exists in America. In other words, he says, a celebration of the magnificent, sensual old is embodied in the very way of life in Europe.

He also thinks it's not so much that European men find a broader range of women sexy but rather that the "women find *themselves* sexy and hold themselves and project themselves in that way." His personal experience—both his ex-wife and his current girlfriend "have spent a couple of Ferraris over the years on their hair"—leads him to believe that European women dye their hair as much as American women. Although, he says, in

Europe, "tan tights and bad shoes and gaudy makeup are much more likely to be a strike against you than gray hair."

The day after I spoke to Nick, I happened to see a *New York Times* magazine feature on the five great living female masters (mistresses?) of Italian design. There was a full-page close-up portrait of each architect and designer, and they ranged in age from sixty-six to eighty-two. Every single one had gray or white hair. None was remotely the Aunt Bea or Barbara Bush or Queen Elizabeth type. They each looked iconoclastic and powerful and even sexy. The pictures gave me goose bumps.

Is Gray the New Black?

I DON'T WANT to seem crazy, but I'm beginning to think that perhaps the rest of the world is changing, slightly, along with me. Just maybe we're starting to see, in a sober, grown-up, twenty-first-century way, part of a second dawning of a different kind of Age of Aquarius. There are small signs. There are glimmers.

Last year, in *The Devil Wears Prada*, Meryl Streep played an absolutely ungrandmotherly white-haired magazine editor, the personification of stylish glamour. Almost every review made a point of mentioning her hair color, and in the movie narrative, her public alpha-female self-confidence is reinforced by her tacit refusal to submit to the blend-in-with-the-pack camouflage of artificial hair color. According to *Entertainment Weekly*, Streep chose the striking "Cruella De Vil" look herself, saying, "In a business that's all about artifice, I like the pride of having naturally beautiful white hair and not coloring it."

And around the same time, the journalist Beth Frerking, who's forty-nine, wrote in *Slate* about her silver hair. "I started going gray in my late thirties, and ever since, strangers, mostly women, stop me on the street—in department stores, at restaurants, even at church—to remark on my hair. In one recent week, I logged four hair comments: 'You have inspired us here, if you don't do anything else today!' said one attractive middle-aged woman whose dark-brown hair was dyed a bright, coppery red."

Lately in magazines there are, more often than not, advertisements featuring gray-haired models. Last year *Good Housekeeping* published an article called "Amazing Grays," a profile of five women with gray hair, with instructions to help its readers decide whether or not to go gray—almost exactly what the same magazine was doing about artificial hair color a half century ago. And Eve Claxton, a writer in her forties, published a long piece in *Vogue* about the pleasure she takes in being gray. In addition to sharing her own epiphanies, Claxton quoted a French-born Manhattan hairstylist, Alain Pinon: "Gray makes a statement. It stands out; it's edgy. People actually ask, 'Who does your color?'" Pinon regards "showing your silver as a choice and one of the few truly exciting things a woman can do with her hair, a way of breaking taboos."

Exciting. Breaking taboos. A bit of Fifth-Avenue-hairstylist hyperbole, maybe...but he's not wrong. My college friend Mary has never used color and says that strangers often ask if they can touch her salt-and-pepper hair. She says, "It's weird and very similar to when I was pregnant and people wanted to touch my belly."

There are other signs that a trend toward broadening the range of culturally acceptable beauty might just be developing. The 2004 Dove study found that women "felt pressure to try and be that 'perfect' picture of beauty: 63 percent strongly agree that women today are expected to be more attractive than their mother's generation.... More than two-thirds (68 percent) of women strongly agree that 'the media and advertising set an unrealistic standard of beauty that most women can't ever achieve.'... Seventy-five percent...wish the media did a better job of portraying women of diverse physical attractiveness, including age, shape, and size."

And so in 2005, the company began to point directly at that beauty-industry disconnect and simmering dissatisfaction, cheerfully rejecting the Big Lie and embracing candor as their way to distinguish their brand. The ongoing Real Women campaign features images of nonmodels of all ages (indeed, as old as ninety-six), freckled women, gray-haired women, and different-size women. Mike Hemingway, the Ogilvy & Mather creative executive who oversaw the development of the campaign, told me that "what Dove is trying to do is be *inspirational,* not aspirational."

Last year Dove once again made news by running a minute-long television ad called "Evolution," illustrating in minute detail the lengths taken to make a model beautiful for a photo shoot—we saw everything, from lengthening the model's neck to digitally enhancing her eyes. It was extraordinary transparency for a major beauty-products marketing campaign to show. And it became a gigantic Web video phenomenon: the last time I checked, six million people had watched it on YouTube.

And in its most recent authenticity campaign, promoting a new line of products called "Pro-Age" for women over forty, Dove commissioned Annie Leibovitz to photograph women, aged fifty-three to seventy-four, naked. And it is exhilarating to see the women, wrinkles and all. Four of the seven women I've seen in ads have gray hair. The Pro-Age Web site states their mission as follows: "Dove wants to instill a new attitude in the anti-aging category—from negative and fear-driven to affirmative and hope-driven. In doing so, we hope to encourage and inspire more women to see the potential that lies within their skin and hair. And themselves." Sure, the goal is to sell masses of product, but fine with me—we all do need to wash our faces and hair, and it is hugely refreshing to see people who look like me selling those products.

Nike, a marketer known for trying to embody hipness, launched an advertising campaign in 2005 celebrating parts of the body that give women the most angst, with copy lines such as "My butt is big," "I have thunder thighs," and "My shoulders aren't dainty or proportional to my hips. Some say they are like a man's. I say, leave men out of it."

Ugly Betty, the new breakout ABC hit, stars America Ferrera *(Real Women Have Curves)* as Betty Suarez, a frumpy young woman working at a fashion magazine. Betty is the hero. And the world acknowledged Ferrera's performance—earlier this year she won the Golden Globe for Best Comic Actress on Television, and the series won Best Comedy.

And speaking of awards season, the frenzy of media stories concerning Helen Mirren's beauty was unquenchable for weeks. Maybe the world really is waking up and realizing that experience and authenticity can be attractive. And that white or gray hair isn't the *absence* of color but rather its very own rich and vibrant color.

After my piece appeared in *More* in 2005, I was overwhelmed by the feedback. Many dozens of women took the time to write, and they even created a support group for going gray on the More.com message boards, and as I read the letters and posts, I realized that I had, as I'd hoped at the outset, joined a community of women who seemed content with the choices they'd made to be their naturally gray selves.

I believe, with fingers crossed, that all of these media expressions are early signs of a real, intensifying hunger for authenticity. I think change may be afoot.

Really Letting Go

I WANT TO BE CLEAR: I'm *not* a born-again zealot proselytizing for a life of back-to-nature purity and austerity. I remain at least as vain as the next person. I intend to continue spending large sums to have my hair cut and styled. Do I want to look as attractive as I can on my sixtieth birthday? You bet. This is complicated, and I don't propose that there are one-size-fits-all answers or absolute litmus tests about living authentically. Nor do I think the choices are all or nothing. Things happen. How we choose to grow older is deeply idiosyncratic, a matter of individual taste and circumstance—depending on one's age, romantic status, professional situation, class, race, ethnicity, geography, all of it.

On New Year's Eve 2005, halfway through my fake-brown-to-real-gray transformation, working out on an elliptical exercise machine in a gym in Naples, Florida, I had another epiphany of sorts—that my yearlong process of letting my hair go gray could be a guiding metaphor for how I wanted to start living my life in general.

I am a total control freak, bordering on OCD—from my workouts, to very neatly made beds, to how I load the dishwasher. I force my household to eat three regularly scheduled, attractive, three-food-group meals a day, and I never let my husband drive the car when I'm in it. And so on. It unquestionably comes from having a perfectionist mother (don't we all?), whom I felt I could never quite satisfy. A decade of therapy gave me that understanding—but not the strength to ratchet down my own control freakishness. So I bumbled along with the guiding principle that if I could control everything that was controllable, then I'd never have to worry about disappointing my mother (may she rest in peace) or anyone else, for that matter. And perfectly dyed hair was such an easily obtainable form of control.

As completely stupid and superficial as it sounds, I realized on that treadmill that if I could allow my hair to be its natural gray, maybe I could learn to be a bit more accepting and easygoing in the rest of my life, too. I could stop clinging to things simply because they were longtime habits. Not making the bed every once in a while probably wouldn't cause the whole house to descend into chaos. Ordering in take-out dinners here or there didn't mean the kids would become sluggish, beer-swilling dropouts. And getting my long, newly gray hair cut to an easier, lighter, graceful length would be okay, too.

It became all of a piece for me: easier and more honest and less-is-more in every aspect of my life. My hair was leading the way because it was so obvious, a 24-7 symbol of making a choice to be direct, clear, and candid.

When I first started allowing my hair to grow out its natural, forty-nine-year-old color, I worried that when I saw people I hadn't seen in a long time, they'd think that I'd "let myself go." It was a reflexive anxiety, one that had nothing to do with what was important to me and everything to do with prepackaged cultural norms of how I was supposed to think about aging. It is assumed among the majority of my peers that a woman entering her sixth decade should attempt to disguise the slightest sign of aging with pretty much every tool at her disposal. If going gray is a sign of "letting yourself go," then the converse must be true — choosing to spend a couple of hours a week on this particular chore is a sign of self-esteem, discipline, and social engagement. Of the people who took my national survey, 6 percent of the women and twice as many men did indeed think — and were un-PC enough to say — that women who go gray are "letting themselves go."

Yet I've come to understand that giving up the relentless $200 trips to the colorist has been, in fact, all about letting go — not in the standard pejorative sense but in dropping the baggage of forever-young anxieties, jettisoning a uniform I no longer feel like wearing.

Once I made the choice to do things differently and began closely observing the women (and men) whom I found the most impressive and alluring, I realized that they were those who seemed the most comfortable in their own skins and who seemed to be striving the least. Great posture, enthusiasm for lots of different kinds of people and places and activities, an instinct for candor, and a twinkle in the eye are vastly more attractive to me than the most perfect, high-sheen, smoothed-out, nipped, tucked, and lacquered look. I know Carmen Dell'Orefice, Frances McDormand, Susanna Moore, Emmylou Harris, Anna Quindlen, and Mireille Guiliano are all subject to the same vain worries (face, boobs, ass, wrinkles, fat, hair) as the rest of us, but they're also all women who sizzle with passion and self-love and a kind of visceral pizzazz, who don't seem *beset* by anxiety over what people think about the ways they look.

I've come to understand that I really don't want to look like some majority-approved standard-issue version of age fifty or fifty-five or sixty or sixty-five—our real-life *Twilight Zone* model Number Twelve. The ways in which my hair changes color and my face wrinkles are unique to me. Why would I want to trade that away to look like some generic version of womanhood? You can't erase what's happened to you in the past or avoid what's really going on now—so why not look it in the eye and accept it?

I ALSO DISCOVERED through further reading that this willingness to allow the world to see me as I am is actually *healthy.* Betty Friedan's exhaustive 1993 study of aging, *The Fountain of Age,* was inspiring. She wrote that "an accurate, realistic, active identification with one's own aging—as opposed both to resignation to the stereotype of being 'old' and denial of age changes — seems an important key to vital aging, and even longevity." The scholarly literature, she found, showed that

An active, realistic acceptance of age-related changes — as opposed to denial or passive resignation — was thus the key to a continued vital involvement in life, a very different face of age than disengagement and decline.... Mindless conformity to the standards of youth can prohibit further development, and that denial can become mindless conformity to the victim-decline model of age. It takes a conscious breaking out of youthful definitions, for a man or woman — to free oneself for continued development in age.

Friedan also discussed the work of Margaret Clark of the Langley Porter Neuropsychiatric Institute in San Francisco, who found that "those who held most tenaciously to certain values of their youth were the most likely candidates for psychiatric breakdown in age. The self-esteem of the healthy older group seemed linked to 'the fruitfulness of a search for meaning in one's life in the later years,' as compared to the mentally ill, who were still pursuing the values of their youth. The healthy group had 'a broader perspective, which they call by different names: wisdom, maturity, peacefulness, or mellowing.'"

Andrew Weil's take in his recent book *Healthy Aging* is similar: "If aging is written into the laws of the universe, then acceptance of it must be a prerequisite for doing it in a graceful way. Yet nonacceptance of aging seems to be the rule in our society, not the exception. A great many people try to deny its reality and progress. Two of the most obvious ways of doing so are the use of cosmetics products and cosmetic surgery." His ultimate conclusion is that to deny aging is to deny ourselves access to a deeply nourishing experience. "Because aging reminds us of our own mortality, it can be a primary stimulus to spiritual awakening and growth."

Bingo! My whole experience hasn't been just about letting my hair grow in its natural gray. It's been about growing *up* and — pardon the touchy-feely cliché — continuing to evolve as a person. By insisting on having hair that looked like it did when I was thirty and thirty-five, I think I really had been forfeiting one of the most important tools for optimal aging — that is, facing it squarely, accepting it incrementally. I think that each year, as my hair becomes whiter, I will be a little more ready to celebrate the good things about my "here and now." I have every intention of avoiding the frail, frightened, old-lady stereotype — to remain as fit and curious as possible — but I am no longer afraid to show my true age. It's simple. I'm proud of what I've done, the years I've lived, how far I've come. I'm happier going through each day — on the sidewalk, in stores and restaurants, at parties — being as honest as I can be about who I really am.

She's letting herself go. I'm trying, anyhow. Letting go of false fronts and mass-market expectations. Letting go for me is all about — self-help alert — finding myself. It's letting go of the need to feel as if it's important to look as much as possible like everyone else. It's letting go of an unsustainable and ultimately counterproductive image of what a fifty-year-old should look like. It's letting go of crutches I don't need—giving up artificial hair color, like giving up cigarettes and booze, is about taking real, personal control of and responsibility for my life, refusing to live according to a script dictated by my own neuroses and marketers' needs to sell stuff. Letting myself go feels okay.

IN THE LARGER SCHEME of things, how important is the decision to color or not to color one's hair? In our contentious, war-torn, terrorist-crazed, disease-ridden, inequitable, cataclysmically climate-changing world, it's hard to imagine a more superficial topic, literally and figuratively, than hair color. But we are people, all of us, not saints. We worry about and, in our various tiny ways, try to contribute to solutions or salves for the big, profound problems—but we *also* care about how we look.

Even if my ballot for a political candidate will never decide an election, and buying a more fuel-efficient car or using compact fluorescent lightbulbs in my lamps won't stop global warming, I will still vote, still feel better getting thirty-one miles to the gallon, and still rest easier knowing that the lighting in my home will not pump literally tons of greenhouse gases into the atmosphere. One's character is the result of hundreds of ordinary, mundane daily choices. And social and cultural progress are the cumulative result of a billion tiny choices. If each of us tries to tell more of the plain truth in small ways, then maybe we as a society and culture will find it easier to start to recognize and reward the truth in bigger ways. And hair, as ridiculous as our obsession with it may be, is a very real, visible, emotionally central sign of what each of us is trying to be—a sort of personal flag. To dye or not to dye, that is *a* question.

Acknowledgments

My entire adult life, I've lived with an extraordinary writer, my husband, Kurt Andersen. And half of the people we know are wonderful writers or editors. So when a few years ago I began to write for a living, I did so with great anxiety. Kurt was generous and supportive beyond belief. Danica Kombol and Akiko Busch have been my advisers and editors throughout. Joanna Coles and Peggy Northrop instantly understood the value of my going gray and encouraged me to write about it for *More* magazine. And my agent, Suzanne Gluck, had the audacity to think that I could write a book, and then sold it. Without all of these people, I would not have had the courage to do this.

At Little, Brown, Judy Clain has been an absolute delight, and Michael Pietsch has been extraordinary — both true partners in the project.

Maira Kalman, of course, took the picture that started the

whole journey. My daughters, Kate and Lucy, have been sweethearts, listening to and supporting me the whole way. Barbara Kass earns a special award for most game friend. Diana Rhoten lent me the intellectual rigor to create the survey, and Rachel Tronstein provided the analytical skills to interpret the data. And I depended upon the generous help of Kay Allaire, Kristi Andersen, Isabelle Anderson, Alice Arlen, Joseph Artale, Andrea Barnett, Mark Beckelman, Elizabeth Beier, Maria Campbell, Ann Carlsen, Mary Chatham, Sophie Cottrell, Carol Davidson, Carmen Dell'Orefice, Nora Ephron, Chris Fanning, Deborah Feingold, Bruce Feirstein, Carin Goldberg, David Good, Mark Grenside, Mireille Guiliano, Cathy Hamilton, Hazel Hammond, Tom Harbeck, Emmylou Harris, John Heilemann, Mike Hemingway, Carla Hendra, Allison Henry, Jade Hobson, Deborah Krulewitch, Ann La Farge, Silvia Lagnado, Karen Landry, Gerry Laybourne, Julianna Lee, Jeffrey Leeds, Susan Lehman, Lynn Lehmkuhl, Ellen Levine, Wendy Lewis, Guy Martin, Pat Mastandrea, Frances McDormand, Sandi Mendelson, Isaac Mizrahi, Seth Mnookin, Susanna Moore, Susan Morrison, Emily Oberman, Lawrence O'Donnell, Elise O'Shaughnessy, George and Sertac Ozrulay, Priscilla Painton, Mary Kay Place, Inge Pumberger, Anna Quindlin, Governor Ann Richards, Heather Rizzo, Linda Schupack, Fred Seibert, Bonnie Siegler, Kiki Smith, Sally Smith, Steve Smith, Lauren Solomon, Emily Thompson, Emily Thorson, Andrea Vazzano, Ellen White, Lauren Zalaznick; my sister, Jane Meyer; and the whole Andersen clan. I am deeply grateful to all.

About the Author

Anne Kreamer is the former executive vice president and world-wide creative director of Nickelodeon / Nick at Nite, and part of the founding team behind *Spy* magazine. She previously created and wrote the monthly American Treasures column for *Martha Stewart Living* and a monthly culture column for *Fast Company.* Kreamer graduated from Harvard College and lives in Brooklyn with her husband, the writer Kurt Andersen, and her two daughters.